Getting IT Right

information and communication technology

Skills Book 2 | Levels 4–5

Alison Page and Tristram Shepard

First published in 1999 by:
Stanley Thornes (Publishers) Ltd

Reprinted in 2002 by:
Nelson Thornes Ltd
Delta Place
27 Bath Road
CHELTENHAM
GL53 7TH
United Kingdom

A catalogue record for this book is available from the British Library.

ISBN 0 7487 4423 1

05 06 07 08 / 10 9

Designed and typeset by Krystyna Hewitt
Artwork by Oxford Designers & Illustrators and John Fowler
Printed and bound in China by Midas Printing International Ltd.

Acknowledgements

The authors would like to acknowledge, with thanks, the assistance of Carol Webb in checking the content of this book.

The following are trademarks of Microsoft Corporation: *Windows 3.0, Windows 3.1, Windows 95, Windows 98, Windows NT, PowerPoint, Outlook Express, Encarta*. Screen shots of all Microsoft products are reprinted with permission from Microsoft Corporation.

Apple and Macintosh are trademarks of Apple Computer, Inc.

Corel and Corel*DRAW* are trademarks or registered trademarks of Corel Corporation or Corel Corporation Limited. Screen shots are © 1999 Corel Corporation and Corel Corporation Limited, reprinted by permission.

Mach Turtles *Logo* is a trademark of Mach Turtles Software Inc.

Yahoo is a registered trademark of Yahoo Inc.

The publishers are grateful to the following for permission to reproduce photographs or other illustrative material:
Ace Photolibrary: pp.8 (right), 128 (PLI)
Advertising Archives: p.23 (right)
Art Directors and TRIP Photolibrary: pp.6 (H Rogers),
7 (top - H Rogers)
BBC logos are reproduced by permission of the BBC: pp.24, 25
Byrotech Data Acquisition: p.76
Cussons (UK): p.77 (bottom)
David Marx: p.134 (middle)
Infogrames: p.64 (right)
John Birdsall Photography: p.37
John Walmesley Photolibrary: pp.7 (bottom), 100
LEGO Dacta: p.68
Martyn Chillmaid: pp.26, 31, 40, 53, 108 (left), 133, 134 (top), 137
Montparnasse Multimedia: p.79
NASA: p.77 (top)
Nissan (Sunderland): p.65
Novalogic: p.64 (left)
Ronald Grant Archive: p.121 (Feature Film Company)
Science Photolibrary: pp.106 (Philippe Plailly),107 (bottom – Sheila Terry)
Sony Broadcast Professional: p.108 (right)
Sony Music Entertainment (UK) Ltd: p.134 (bottom)
Stockmarket: p.8 (left)
Swindon Borough Council: p.122
Telegraph Colour Library: p.135
The Velux Company Ltd: p.22
Warner Music (UK) Ltd: p.23 (left)

All other photographs from NT Archive.

Every effort has been made to contact copyright holders. The publishers apologise to anyone whose rights have been overlooked and will be happy to rectify any errors or omissions at the earliest opportunity.

Contents

Getting IT Right

Welcome to Getting IT Right Book 2! This book will help you to extend your skills in using information and communication technologies.

On Target

If you are using Book 2 you should already know the basics of using computers. You should also already have some experience with the different types of software.

In this book you will revise some of the things you know and can do already. This will help to make you more capable and confident.

At the same time you will learn more about:

■ how to **use** what you know

■ how to **apply** your skills to getting things done.

You will also learn some new skills, to extend the ways that you can use computers and other electronic technologies.

About the units

The book starts with a short introductory section called *Starting Up*. It is then divided into ten units. Each unit is based on a different software package. You may not have exactly the same package used in the illustrations but you are sure to have something very similar. Your teacher will tell you about any important differences.

Each unit starts with its own introduction. This helps to explain the sort of everyday problems and situations in which you are likely to find it helpful to use IT. The introduction also makes it clear what the targets for the unit are, that is what you should know about and be able to do by the time you have worked through the unit.

You will also find some suggestions for how you might use the software in your other subjects.

If you have used **Getting IT Right** Book 1 you will find that you are already familiar with the way that this book is laid out. There are only a few differences, such as:

● the introduction sections to most units are longer, to ensure you understand more about how to apply what you learn to using IT to solve problems

● there are ten units, instead of nine. The extra unit, on databases, is at the end of the book, so all the other units use the same number and colour as Book 1.

For those of you who are new to **Getting IT Right**, the rest of this page summarises some of the main features of the units and gives you an idea of what to expect.

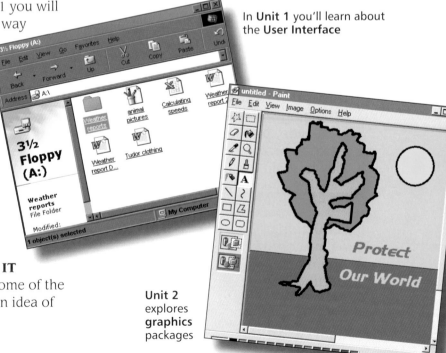

In **Unit 1** you'll learn about the **User Interface**

Unit 2 explores **graphics** packages

What you have to do ■

Work through the numbered pages in each unit in order. In some lessons you might get through several pages quite quickly, especially if you've used a similar package before. Or maybe it's been quite a while since you last used a particular piece of software. You might find some of the early pages very useful for revision.

Each double-page spread is self-contained. Read it through first, or listen carefully as your teacher takes you through it. The next step is to experiment with the various actions needed to make the program work, such as:

● finding menus
● clicking in the right place
● dragging things across the screen.

It takes a while to get used to some of these!

In particular, look out for instructions on the page which follow coloured buttons. For example:

● Click on **New** in the **File** menu

Make sure you try these things out.

On most right-hand pages you'll find a very important section in the bottom corner called *What you have to do.* These are activities you should do after you have experimented for a while, and have got to know what you're doing. Your teacher will tell you which ones to do – some might be done after the lesson, and others are for those who are speeding ahead.

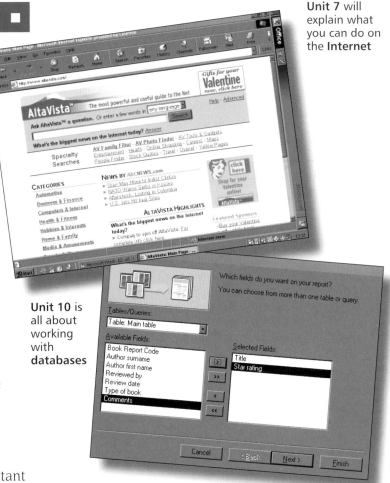

Unit 7 will explain what you can do on the **Internet**

Unit 10 is all about working with **databases**

Controlling things is the subject of **Unit 5**

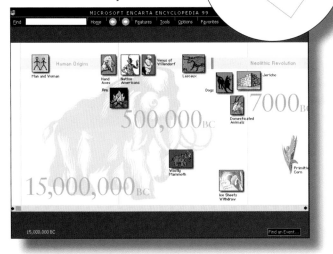

Unit 6 is all about how to find things out

Always remember to save the work you do on the computer. You should also print out your work as often as possible. Keep it in a special IT folder.

At the end of each unit your teacher will probably give you a special project to undertake. You'll be given a problem to solve and will be expected to use the computer to help you. To begin with you'll need to plan out what you need to do and when. At the end you'll need to evaluate your work.

This project will help you and your teacher to work out how well you are doing. It will show up your strengths and weaknesses, and provide you with some useful targets for improvement in the next unit you do.

You can apply what you learn in this book to all your school subjects. Don't wait for your teachers to tell you to use the technology. Can you see a way in which using a computer or some other electronic device would help you to get the job done better? Don't hesitate to ask if you can do it that way!

Good luck with your work – we hope you manage to *Get IT Right!*

I. Making changes

This book is about how computers can help you with your schoolwork. Read this page for an overview of how school life has changed since computers were introduced.

Introduction

Not so long ago there were no computers in schools. Very few families had a computer at home.

But all that has changed. Nowadays everyone uses computers at school to help them with their work. And computer use is going to increase even more.

This book will help you to make the most of the computers at school and at home. In it you will learn many different ways of using computers and you will see how computers can help you with your schoolwork in all subjects.

Working IT out

At one time all calculations were worked out by hand.

Computers can be used to calculate results, for example in maths and science. Save the time you would spend on boring and repetitive calculation. Spend more time and effort on the challenging and interesting side of the task.

Making IT artistic

You don't necessarily have to use pen, paper and paint to create a work of art.

Free the artist inside. Computers can give you control over colour and design. They can help you to make changes and corrections to your artwork. Even if you aren't confident in your drawing ability, you can use computers to make your design ideas come true.

Finding IT out

Books are an important source of information. Computers won't replace books but they do provide you with an extra resource.

An important part of modern education is that you have to learn to find things out for yourself. The teacher won't always give you the answers. Sometimes it's up to you. Computers give you a powerful new way to find things out.

Find things out from CD-ROMs which are computer disks stocked full of words, pictures, sound and video. Find things out from the Internet, a world-wide network of computers that you can use to search for information on any topic under the sun.

Putting IT in writing

At one time all schoolwork was written by hand using pen and paper.

Computers can help you to make your written work neat, accurate and well presented. This leaves you free to concentrate on the most important task – working out what to write and how to express it in words.

Creating IT

Computers have opened up new types of creativity which didn't exist before.

You will learn to use all kinds of software packages in this book. But how is software made? Learn how to write simple computer programs. Create a new computer game and look at some of the creative ideas that games programmers bring to their work.

Presenting IT to an audience

Flip charts, transparencies, *chalk and talk*. These are the old ways of communicating with an audience.

Use computers to combine words and pictures into attractive documents. Use words and images to persuade, advertise or argue a case.

Create on-line presentations which you can display to the audience while you are giving your talk.

Communicating IT far and wide

At school you learn how to write letters. But nowadays there are other ways of communicating.

Using e-mail you can communicate with other people all over the world in a matter of seconds. In this book you will learn how to use e-mail connections to communicate.

Storing IT

Information that you have written on pieces of paper or organised into an exercise book. This used to be the only way you could store the facts you learned.

In science, history, geography and other subjects, you collect information. You can use computers to store this information.

Computers will store facts in an organised way, making it easy for you to keep information safe and come back to it when you need it.

WHAT YOU HAVE TO DO

Talk to your parents, or other adults, about what they used to do at school. Write down at least three ways that schools have changed due to new technology since then.

Discuss what you have found out with the other people in your class.

2. Taking care with IT

On this page you will look at good working practice when using information and communication technologies.

Work with care

No matter what use you make of computers, you should work with **care** and **attention** to minimise damage and danger.

Good working practice should be shown at all times, no matter what you are using computers to do.

If you learn good working practice now, you will find it will help you

- at school and college
- at home
- in any job you do.

Caring for the human user

The most important part of the computer system is the human user. It is part of your job to care for that user – whether it is you or somebody else.

Here are some of the things you should do:

- look after your own health – for example, be careful about electricity, and don't work for hours and hours without a break
- look after other people – the computer room is often busy and crowded. Work so that you don't annoy anyone else
- encourage a good working atmosphere – make sure everyone feels comfortable and safe in the computer room
- share and co-operate – often there isn't enough computer equipment and you have to share. This can be difficult for everyone. It is your responsibility to work with generosity and goodwill.

Caring for equipment

It is in everyone's interest to take good care of the computers you use. If they are broken then there are fewer to go round. You are more likely to have to share or wait.

Some people worry that they can break a computer by typing the wrong thing. But you aren't going to wreck a computer that way.

The most common way to break a computer is to spill a drink into it. Food is pretty bad too. Never eat or drink while you are sitting at the computer.

Knocking a computer off the table, putting a chair through the screen and other kinds of major breakage are very easy to avoid. Simply treat the equipment with a little bit of care.

Caring for software ■

Modern software is *robust*. That means you can't do any permanent damage to a computer package just by using it.

The main risk to the software and information held on computers is from computer *viruses*. Viruses are hidden computer programs. They are transferred by mistake from computer to computer when you copy software.

A virus on a computer system can destroy the software and information held on the computer. It won't break the computer but it can mean the loss of the work stored on the computer.

Do your best to keep viruses off the computers at school. Never, ever, copy software onto the computer system at school. You should also try to keep viruses off your own computer at home if you have one. Don't take copies of software from friends because they might pass on a virus by accident.

Care for your work ■

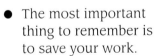

Your work might not be worth a lot of money – but it is precious to you. You have probably put a lot of time and effort into your computer work.

● The most important thing to remember is to save your work.

Save your work as a computer file. Save it regularly during the lesson – don't wait until the end.

● The next important thing to remember is to make a backup.

Make a copy of any computer file you use. Save the copy onto a spare disk and put it somewhere safe.

Where to save? ■

Save your work onto a floppy disk or on the school network. Don't tell anyone else your network password.

Your teacher may tell you not to save your work onto the hard disk of the computer in the classroom. It might not be safe there. When you come back the next day your work might be gone.

If you do use the hard disk to save your work, remember to sit at exactly the same computer in the next lesson in order to load the work you have saved.

Don't worry - I won't bite!

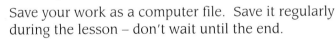

WHAT YOU HAVE TO DO

1. **What are the rules about working in your school computer room? Get a copy and put it in your IT folder. If there is no official document then sit down and write one with your teacher.**

2. **As a class look over the rules that are in place. Would you change them or add to them? Do the rules do enough to make sure that everyone in your school is safe and comfortable using the computer?**

1

The User Interface

In this unit you will learn about the Windows system, which helps you to use the computer.

On Target

The **Windows** system allows you to make use of computer software to do work. You should already know:

- the common features of a Windows interface
- how to start up software packages
- how to copy and delete work files
- how to save and print.

In this unit you will revise these skills and learn to:

- use multiple packages
- use the **clipboard** to copy and paste
- use folders to manage your files.

You can work through this unit now if you wish, or you can use it as a reference resource, as you work through the other units in this book.

Starting programs

The main thing you might want to do with the desktop is start up programs. There are three main ways to do this.

- Double-click a software icon.
- Double-click a work file icon.
- Use the Start button.

You will have started up packages before. Make sure you know about all three methods.

Icons

You might see icons like these on the desktop. Icons like this can stand for software packages, work files, or other computer functions – for example the recycle bin.

The desktop

When you start work with the computer you see a screen called the **Desktop**. The appearance of the desktop is not fixed. The appearance of the desktop is not fixed. The person who is in charge of the computer can make lots of decisions about what it looks like.

Here is one desktop from a computer. The person who set up this desktop has put a background picture on it. The background picture is called the **Wallpaper**. (Wallpaper on a desktop? Who said computers were logical?). Your computer will certainly have different wallpaper from this, but you may see many of the same features.

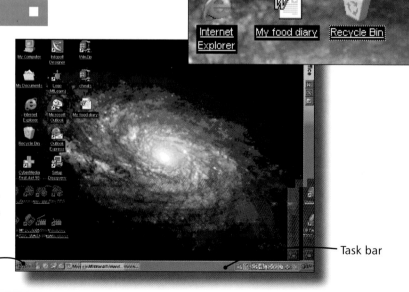

Task bar

Start button

i   Variations *p12*   The typical window *p14*   Create a folder *p21*

Folders

You won't find all the icons on the desktop. Some are held in folders. Folders look like this.

Folders can hold lots of icons.

● Double-click a folder to open it up

It opens as a window and you can see the icons inside it. Folders can also hold other folders. You can learn more about folders on page 23.

Start button

The **Start** button is in the lower left hand corner.

● Click on the Start button to open the Start menu

Near the top of the Start Menu you will see the option **Programs**.

● Click on this option to open the programs menu

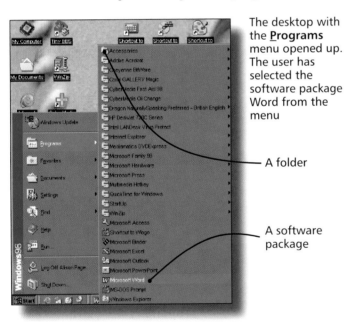

The desktop with the **Programs** menu opened up. The user has selected the software package Word from the menu

— A folder

— A software package

You can pick the software package you want from this menu. The menu also contains folders.

● Click on the name of the folder to see more software packages

Task bar

The task bar shows all the software packages that are open at the moment. Click on the buttons on the task bar to swap between these software packages.

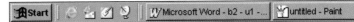

Close a package

When you open a package it starts in its own window. You may already know about the main features of a software window, and there are more details later in this unit. However if you don't have time to do any more work in this lesson, simply close down the packages you open.

● Click on the **X** in the top right hand corner of the window to close a package

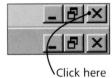

Click here

Click or double-click?

To **Open** a file or a package from an icon you normally **double-click** it. That means click twice in quick succession. However, some modern computers have been set up so that you only have to click an icon once to open it.

You will quickly learn which of these two methods works on your computer. Adapt what it says on this page to whichever type of system you have.

WHAT YOU HAVE TO DO

1. **Look at the desktop of the computer you use at school. Answer these questions.**

■ **What software package icons are shown?**

■ **What work file icons are shown?**

■ **What folders are shown on the desktop?**

   If the desktop is very crowded with icons, pick just three from each category.

2. **Use the Start button to start up a software package, or open one up from the desktop. Then close the package down.**

I. Windows on the world

No matter what user interface you use at school, you can work successfully with the computer. On this page you will look at some different windows interfaces.

Variations

The examples in this unit were all created using the **Microsoft** *Windows 98* operating system. This is not the only operating system that is available.

The differences between operating systems are not as important as the great similarities between them. All of the work in this book can be done using any of the common operating systems. However, if you are puzzled by the differences between what you see on your computer at school and the pictures in this book, then this page will help you.

Networks

One difference that might affect you is if your computer is joined to a school **network**.

The main difference if you are joined to a network is that you will have access to extra storage areas from your desktop. The exact system will depend on how the network is set up at school. Your teacher will explain it to you.

There is a special network operating system called Microsoft *Windows NT* but, for the ordinary user (like you), it works in much the same way as any other Windows system.

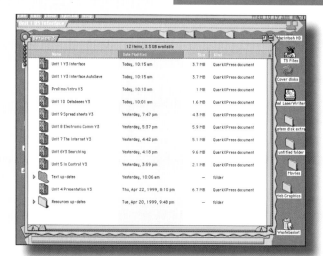

Windows 95

Microsoft *Windows 95* is a very similar operating system to *Windows 98*. Here is a window from *Windows 95*.

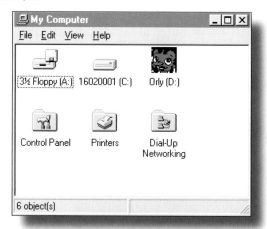

The same methods can be used in both systems to start up packages, work in software windows and manage files. You shouldn't have any difficulty in following the work in this book using *Windows 95*.

Apple Macintosh

Apple Macintosh computers are often favoured by people who use their computer for artistic or creative tasks. These were the earliest computers to feature a graphical interface, with icons and a mouse pointer. The operating system is very similar to the Windows system.

Windows 3.x

Before *Windows 95* there was a different type of Windows operating system. There were several versions of this early type of Windows, and together these are called *Windows 3.x*. Read this section if you are using this type of computer system.

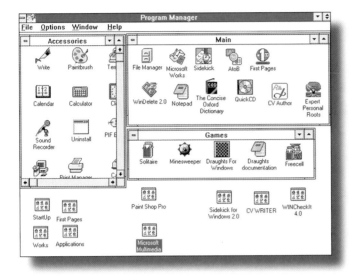

You shouldn't have too much trouble following the work in this book if you use a *Windows 3.x* system. However, you might find the software packages that are available are a little old-fashioned and lack some of the features of modern Windows software.

Here are the main differences you should bear in mind:

- folders are called directories
- there are icons for software packages but not for work files
- there is no Start button or task bar at the bottom of the screen.

Because of these differences you can only start up a package in one way – by finding the software icon and double-clicking on it.

Because there are no icons for work files you can't do file management tasks by dragging files on the desktop. Instead you must use a special software package called *File Manager* which lists your files and lets you do tasks like copy and delete.

Because there is no task bar you can't click on task bar buttons to swap between open packages. Instead you have to:

- hold down the **ALT** key
- press the **TAB** key.

Web style

An interesting feature of *Windows 98* is that it can be set up to run in different ways. So your system at school might look a bit different from the examples in this unit.

One of the main differences this makes has been mentioned on the last page. Depending on how the system has been set up, you might open up software packages, folders and work files by clicking on them once instead of twice.

Another difference is the way that folder windows are presented. On the last page you saw that when you click on a drive or folder it opens as a window. When you are working in *web style* this doesn't happen. Instead the new storage location opens in the same window.

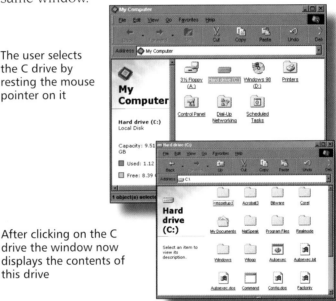

The user selects the C drive by resting the mouse pointer on it

After clicking on the C drive the window now displays the contents of this drive

As only one folder window is open at a time you move between them using the **Back** and **Forward** buttons.

WHAT YOU HAVE TO DO

1. **Which operating system do you use at school? Do you use any different operating systems on other computers at school or at home?**

2. **Write a short note about the operating system(s) you use and put it in your IT folder.**

2. File it

On this page you will look at the features of a typical software window. You will also see how to save, open and print files from within the typical window.

Software package window

All packages within the **Windows** operating system work in much the same way. This is handy because it makes it easier to learn new packages.

The typical window ■

Here is the window of a typical package, showing the main features.

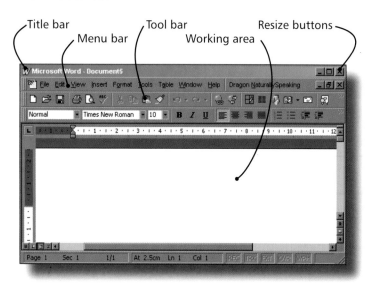

Title bar
Menu bar
Tool bar
Working area
Resize buttons

The title bar shows the name of the package. The menu bar shows the title of each menu, which you can open by clicking. The tool bar has icons that stand for software features. The working area is where your work will appear.

Resize buttons ■

You probably already know how the **resize** buttons work.

Shrink to a button
Shrink to half size
Close completely

On most packages there are two lots of buttons. The lower set affect the working area, and the file held in it. The upper set of buttons affect the entire software package and the whole window.

Using the software package you can shrink the window to a button on the task bar, or resize it to half or full screen size, or close it down altogether.

Working with files ■

The work you create in a software package is called a **file**. There are three main actions you can take with files:

New file
Open file

● start a new blank file
● save the file
● open a file you made before.

Save file

These three actions are usually available as icons on the tool bar. Click on the icon to pick the action.

If you use a software package that does not have these icons on the tool bar, the same choices are available in the **File** menu.

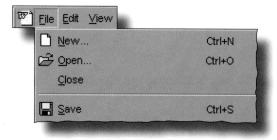

Pick a file

If you choose to **open** a file then you will have to pick the file you want to open. You will see a window like this.

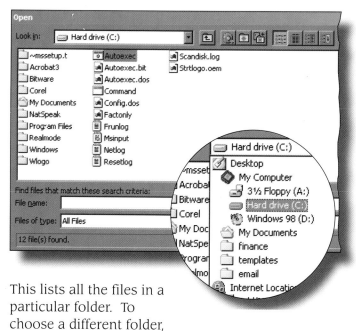

This lists all the files in a particular folder. To choose a different folder, open the menu at the top of the window.

From this menu you can choose between different storage areas, and select folders within the storage areas. The files in the selected folder are listed in the window. Pick the file you want, and click on the **Open** button.

Save details

The first time you **save** your work as a file you will see a similar window.

Pick a storage area and folder

Type a file name

Click here

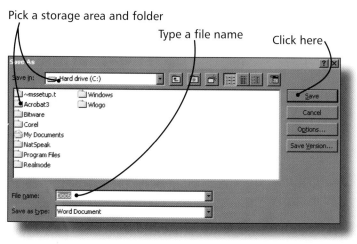

Use it in a similar way to the *Open* window except that you have to type in a new file name.

Save again, save as...

As you saw on page 9 it is a good idea to save your file repeatedly as you work, for security. Click on the **Save** symbol whenever you like. This will quickly save the file, using the same storage location and file name that you selected the first time you saved it.

If you want to save the file using a different file name or storage location, use the option **Save As...** in the **File** menu. This brings up the **Save** window again, so you can change the save options.

Print

The other thing you do with your work is to **print** it out. There is usually a print icon on the tool bar. But if this isn't available, pick **Print...** from the **File** menu.

If you click on the print icon your work will go straight to the printer. If you pick **Print...** from the menu you will see a window, something like this one.

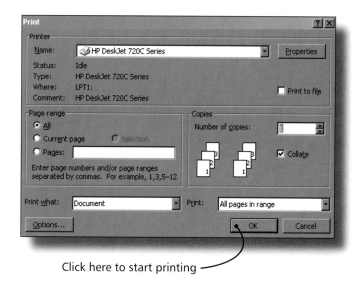

Click here to start printing

If you have a choice of printer you might be able to pick between them from this window. Your teacher will tell you how printing is set up in your school.

WHAT YOU HAVE TO DO

Open a word processing package and type in your answers to Question 1 on page 11 when you looked at the desktop.

Save and print your work. Keep it in your IT folder.

3. On the clipboard

Here you can review how to copy and paste items using an area of memory called the *clipboard*.

Cut, copy and paste

Your computer has a special area of electronic memory set aside for temporary storage. This piece of memory is called the **clipboard**. You can use the clipboard to store items that you want to copy or move.

The clipboard is electronic memory. You cannot look at it. You cannot see the items that are stored there.

On this page you will cover:

- how to use the clipboard
- how using the clipboard can help with your work.

You can use the clipboard with almost every type of software. You will use the methods you learn on this page in many of the units that follow.

An electronic clipboard is rather like a real clipboard. It's easy to clip a piece of paper with text and/or pictures onto it, take it off again and then clip on something different.

Select and highlight

Before you can transfer an item of work to the clipboard you have to **select** it. In most packages you select an item by dragging the mouse pointer over it.

The selected item could be:

- a group of words
- a range of spreadsheet cells
- part of a picture.

When the item is selected it is usually highlighted as black on white.

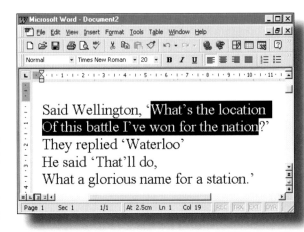

Part of the limerick has been selected and is highlighted

In other cases, highlighted items are marked out with a border or with square handles.

One of the octopus' eyes has been selected and is marked with square handles

← *i* Copy and paste *p31*   Copy text *p42*

Put into the clipboard ■

Once an item is selected it can be put onto the clipboard. There are two ways to do this.

● **Cut** – the item is removed from where it is and put onto the clipboard.
● **Copy** – the item remains where it is, and a copy is put onto the clipboard.

You *can't see the clipboard*. You have to remember what you have **cut** or **copied** onto the clipboard. The clipboard only stores one item at a time. If you use **cut** or **copy** a second time then the new item will replace what was already on the clipboard.

Take from the clipboard ■

Once an item is stored on the clipboard you can **paste** it into your work. **Paste** means that whatever is on the clipboard is copied into the current working area.

Tool bar icons ■

The three actions – cut, copy and paste – are shown in most packages by **tool bar icons**. Click one of these to carry out the action.

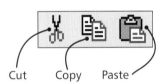

Cut   Copy   Paste

Other methods ■

Some packages don't have these icons. You can cut, copy and paste in other ways.

Use the keyboard
● To **Copy** – hold down the **Control** key and press the **C** key.
● To **Cut** – hold down the **Control** key and press the **X** key.
● To **Paste** – hold down the **Control** key and press the **V** key.

Use the menu system

Cut, **Copy** and **Paste** are all options in the **Edit** menu of every package.

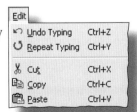

How the clipboard helps ■

Moving
Use the clipboard to move an item to a new place.

● Cut it from where it was.
● Paste it in the new location.

Multiple copies
You can paste an item from the clipboard over and over again. In this way you can put lots of copies of the same item into your work.

Between packages
On page 11 you saw how you could open more than one package and swap between them. You can use the clipboard to copy an item from one package to another.

For example, you can create a graphic and copy it onto the clipboard. Next you can swap to a word processed document and paste that graphic into the document.

In this way you can combine several types of work into one document.

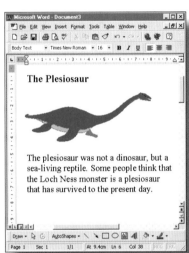

On page 11 you saw

WHAT YOU HAVE TO DO

Answer the following questions.

1. What do you have to do to an item before you can put it onto the clipboard?

2. What are the two ways of putting items onto the clipboard, and what is the difference between them? Describe any advantages or disadvantages of each method.

3. Describe two ways you can tell the computer to paste an item from the clipboard into your work.

Keep your answers in your IT folder.

4. Organise my computer (I)

You have a storage area where you save your work files. Here you will learn how to organise your files in the storage area.

File management

As you work with software packages you will create files. On these pages you will see how to **manage** the files in your storage area. For example:

- create folders and move files into them
- delete files you no longer need
- rescue files you delete by accident
- make backup copies.

If possible, try to follow some of the work shown on this page in your own storage area.

Your storage area

Where do you save your work files? If you have a computer at home you might use the hard disk (the C drive). At school you might use the C drive, a floppy disk, or perhaps a folder on the school network.

Make sure you know the right storage area to use before you go on with this part of the book.

Using the desktop

From the desktop of your computer you can reach any storage area.

See if you can find these icons on the desktop.

You can use these icons to reach the place where your files are stored.

My Documents

The icon called **My Documents** links you to a folder on the hard disk. The folder is set aside to store work files. You might store files in the **My Documents** folder of your home computer.

In some schools pupils use the **My Documents** folder to store their work. If that's what you do at your school, read this section. If not, you can miss out this section and go on to **My Computer**.

- Double-click on the **My Documents** icon

You will see all the files stored in this folder. It might look something like this.

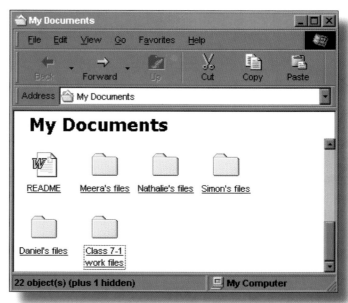

The files might be shown by name, or they might be organised into folders. Ideally there will be a folder with your name on it, where your work files are kept separately from everyone else's.

- Double-click on this folder to see your files

On the next page you will see how to work with these files.

 i The desktop *p10* Icons *p10*

My Computer

The **My Computer** icon opens a window that shows all the storage areas that are available to you.

● Make sure you have closed any open windows and you are looking at the desktop
● Double-click on the **My Computer** icon

You will see a window that looks something like this.

There are icons in the **My Computer** window for every storage area

You have already decided which storage area to use.

● Find the icon for that storage area
● Double-click on the icon

A window opens that shows everything in the storage area. You might see files. You might see folders.

● If your work is stored in a folder, find the folder and open it by double-clicking

Shortcuts to storage areas

On some computers there are shortcuts on the desktop that lead straight to a storage area.

● Close down any windows that are open and look at the desktop. You might see icons like this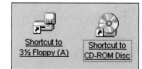

These are shortcuts to the various storage areas.

● Double-click on one of these icons. A window will open showing you what is in that storage area

This is a quick way to access a storage area.

Look at your files

On this page you have seen how to find your files from the desktop:

● you might use the **My Documents** icon
● you might use the **My Computer** icon
● you might use desktop shortcuts to storage areas.

Whichever method you use you will end up looking at a window that shows your work files. It might look something like this.

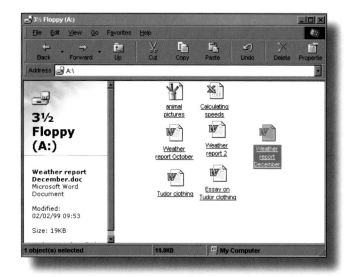

Open files

● Double-click on a file icon. The computer will start up the right software package and open that file

There are other things you can do with files. For example, you can delete them, copy them and move them. Find out more about this on the next page.

5. Organise my computer (2)

Next you will work with the files you have saved. Before you start, close down any open software packages. Your storage area window should be open, but not filling the whole screen.

Delete files ■

One of the actions you might want to take is to delete files that you no longer need.

You can do this by using the **recycle bin**. See if you can find this icon on the desktop.

If the recycle bin is displayed on your computer then you can delete files using this method.

● Look in the window where your files are displayed

● Move the mouse pointer to the file you want to delete

● Hold down the mouse button and drag the file out of the window, across the desktop, and into the recycle bin

The dragged icon looks like a see-through ghost.

If you can't find the recycle bin on the desktop then use this method to delete a file.

● Move the mouse pointer to the file

● Click with the right button of the mouse

You will see this menu

● Pick **Delete** from the menu

Are you sure? ■

Before a file is deleted the computer may double-check to see if you are sure you want to delete it.

● Click **Yes** to confirm that you want to delete the file

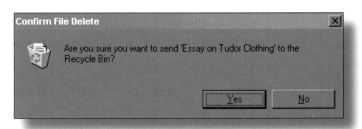

Restore a deleted file ■

If you delete a file by accident you can get it back out of the recycle bin. But only if you deleted it from the permanent storage of your computer. If you delete a file from a floppy disk you can't restore it.

● Double-click on the recycle bin to open it up

You will see all the recently deleted files.

● Select the file you want to rescue from the bin

● Open the **File** menu

● Select **Restore**

The file returns to where it was.

The bin has a limited capacity, and after files have been in there for a while, they will be deleted for good. So don't leave it too long to try and restore a lost file.

Rename files ■

You can change the name of any file in your storage area. Make sure the storage area is open as a window. Find the icon of the file you want to rename.

- Right-click on the file icon

You will see a menu like this.

- Select **Rename** from the menu (it is near the bottom)
- Type a new name for the file

Create a folder ■

You can make new folders in your storage area, and use them to store your files. This makes your storage area more organised, particularly if you have lots of files.

Your storage area should be open as a window. Along the top of this window is a 'menu bar'.

- Open the **File** menu
- Select **New**
- Select **Folder**
- Type in the name of the new folder

In this example the pupil has created a new file called *Weather reports*.

Move files into a folder ■

To tidy your files away into the folders you have made you just drag the file icon into the folder icon.

Copy files to a floppy disk ■

If your files are stored on the hard disk or the network you can easily copy them onto a **floppy disk** as a backup.

Your storage area is open as a window filling part of the screen. Elsewhere on the screen find the icon for the floppy disk. It might be a shortcut on the desktop. Or perhaps you will have to open the My Computer icon as a window (see page 19).

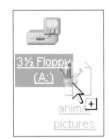

Simply drag the file icon to the floppy disk icon.

On Target

In this unit you have learned about the Windows interface. You should now know how to use Windows to:

- start up software packages
- copy and paste items between packages
- save and print your work
- manage your work files.

WHAT YOU HAVE TO DO

Use the techniques you have learned in this section to complete these tasks.

1. **Create a backup disk holding a copy of each one of your school files.**

2. **Make a new folder in your storage area, with a suitable name, to save all the work you do from this book.**

2 Graphics

In this unit you will learn about how graphics software can be used to create pictures and designs and communicate ideas

On Target

You should already know how to:

- use a range of graphics tools
- use the mouse to draw on the screen
- select and combine features to create graphics.

In this unit you will revise these skills and learn about:

- the two main types of graphics package and how they are used
- how to adapt a design to meet the requirements of a specification
- how to vary the features of a graphic and evaluate the results.

You will look at two different types of graphics package and look at two classroom projects that involve the use of graphics software.

Communicate information

Imagine you want to explain to someone what the British Isles look like, and the positions of the main cities. How difficult that would be in words alone. But show them a map, and it is suddenly clear.

A map uses various *conventions* that we all understand. For example, cities are shown as dots, and the blue area is the sea.

Can you identify five pieces of information shown by this map?

Why use graphics?

There are two main reasons to use graphics in your work:

- to give information
- to make an impression.

Sometimes you want to achieve both of these with one piece of work.

Sometimes it is much easier to give someone the information they need by using a picture or diagram instead of just words.

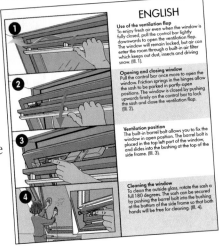

Another way to show information is to provide a more realistic drawing.

The drawing on the left leaves out unwanted details – for example, there are no backgrounds and no unnecessary colours.

Making an impression ■

Graphics can also be used to make your audience feel happy or sad, excited or calm, etc. The use of colour and images can often create an emotional feeling greater than words on their own.

Frequently a graphic includes some information, such as a name. But the way in which the information is shown is at least as important as the information itself.

These album covers show the title of the album and the name of the singer or band. But most importantly they show this information in a way that produces an impression, and tells you what type of music to expect.

Think about the colours and images used in these covers. What impression do these covers give you about the different types of music on the CDs?

Commercial companies use images in advertising and packaging to create an impression in the mind of the customer.

This advert uses colours (red and white) which produce a feeling of Christmas celebration. The colours also relate to the colours on the product label.

In this way the manufacturers hope to associate their own product closely with the idea of celebration and enjoyment.

"For Santa"

The picture of Santa has an emotional impact for most children growing up in countries that celebrate Christmas. All the features of this graphic combine to produce exactly the impression that the manufacturers intend.

Graphics can also be used to produce a humorous reaction. The cartoonist has exaggerated the features of the person on the right to make them easy to recognise. The distortion also makes the person look a bit ridiculous.

www.CartoonStock.com

What impression is this cartoon giving of the person? Does the cartoonist like the person?

Purpose and audience ■

Each image on the previous page was created for a specific **purpose**. Every image was created for a distinct **audience**. The person who made the graphic had to keep the audience and purpose clearly in mind.

For example, the map of the UK had the overall purpose of showing information about the country. The more detailed purpose was to show the regions and cities of the UK, rather than (for example) the mountains, hills and woodlands.

The audience for the map understands basic map making conventions. The person drawing the map could use symbols and techniques to convey information, knowing that these symbols would be understood.

Note down the purpose and audience for every picture shown on these introductory pages.

IT at work

Design and Image

Every organisation wants to have a good image. Companies use design to help create a strong identity. For example there are five terrestrial TV stations in this country. Each station has its own graphic 'logo' which is shown regularly on the air. When you are watching TV you can easily tell which channel you are watching because of the channel logo that appears.

A logo is a distinctive design made from the name of a company or product.

- Why use a logo instead of just saying what channel it is?
- Which TV logo do you like best?
- An interesting graphics exercise is to create a logo for a new TV channel. Redesign one of the logos shown here, or create a logo for 'Channel 6'.

TV channel logos are often generated and played back electronically – they only exist in the memory of a computer. TV companies employ the best computer graphics experts to create images that are both attractive and useful.

How graphics work ■

Graphics convey information by:

- using common conventions understood by the audience
- using realistic pictures
- leaving out unnecessary details.

Graphics produce an impression by:

- use of colour
- use of pictures with emotional content
- distorting or altering pictures.

← _i_ Add text p29

Getting IT Right in...

Geography

Computer graphics can be used in school in any situation where you need a picture or diagram. If you ever find you have to get out your pencil or pen and draw something, you could use computer graphics instead.

For example, a pupil used a graphics package in Geography to produce this diagram of the compostion of soil.

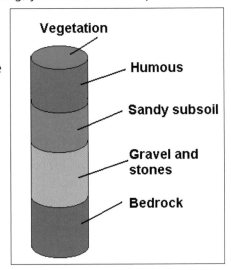

Vegetation

Humous

Sandy subsoil

Gravel and stones

Bedrock

Design and Technology

A group doing a **Graphic Products** task used a computer to help create a board game. They were able to experiment with different colours, shapes and typefaces until they found the ones that worked best.

WHAT YOU HAVE TO DO

As a class, make a collection of graphics. Everyone should bring in at least one example of a graphic – not a photograph – that they have found.

Choose five different examples of graphics. For each graphic describe:

- the information the graphic gives
- the emotional impression given
- the purpose of the graphic
- the audience for which the graphic is intended.

Keep your work in your IT folder.

I. Mug shots (I)

On this page you will look at how a pupil used graphics software to complete a project.

Create graphics

On this page you will look at an example of a graphics project completed using the software package called **Microsoft** *Paint*. You may have used this package before, or one very similar.

You will learn more about how the wide range of graphics tools that are available are used to build up a picture.

Use *Paint*, or a similar simple graphics package, and follow the instructions given here to create your own version of the design.

The project

Charities raise money in many ways. One way is to sell merchandise with the name of the charity on it. An example would be a mug with the name of the charity, and perhaps a suitable design.

A class were given the task of creating a design for the charity *Protect Our World* (POW for short). The design should be suitable for printing onto a mug to sell to raise money for the charity.

The software

The class used the software package *Paint*, which is provided as part of the *Windows* interface.

Start up your *Paint* package:

- Open the **Start** menu
- Open the **Programs** menu
- Open the **Accessories** folder
- Find the *Paint* icon and click on it

The tools

On the left of the *Paint* window is the tool bar. Each icon on this tool bar stands for a graphics tool that you can use to build up a picture. Try to follow the example shown here, using your own software package.

Constructing the picture

The line tool   The paint pot tool   The colour palette

The first step in this design is to split the picture into earth and sky colours.

- Select the **line** tool, and drag across the screen to split it into two
- Select the **paint pot** tool. Pick **brown** from the colour palette. Click below the line to colour that half brown
- Select **sky blue** from the colour palette and click above the line

i   Save details *p15*   Print *p15*

- Next draw the outline of the tree in black using the **brush** tool

The paint brush tool

NB. In this example the *Paint* window is only partial screen size. Use a full-size window when you make your picture. Make sure the tree you draw doesn't take up the whole screen. Make the tree as tall as you like, but leave plenty of room on the right of the screen. You will use this space to add more items later.

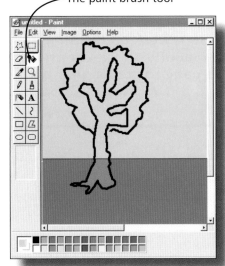

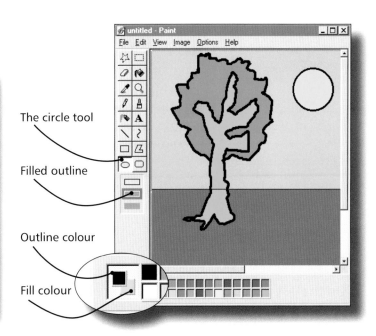

The circle tool

Filled outline

Outline colour

Fill colour

- Use the **paint pot** to add colour to the trunk and leaves

The first time Alice, one of the pupils, tried this it went wrong. The line marking the leaves had a break in it and the colour flooded into the rest of the picture. If a mistake like this happens use **Undo** (in the **Edit** menu) to reverse the change.

Alice did this. Then she filled in the gap in the line and poured colour a second time. This time it worked.

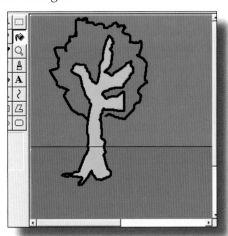

Finally she added the sun. Here is how to do it.

- Select the **circle** tool
- Choose **filled outline** to draw a circle with an outline and an inner colour
- Click on **black** to pick the outline colour
- Right-click on **yellow** to pick the **fill** colour.
- Drag to draw the circle on the screen
- Hold down the **SHIFT** key as you draw to make the shape a perfect circle

Print and save

When she had got this far Alice ran out of time. She saved the work, and printed out a copy. Look on page 15 to see how to print and save a file. There are no tool bar icons for these actions, so you will have to use the keyboard or the menu system.

On the next page you can see how Alice improved the picture and added text to it.

Line and brush style

Alice wanted bold thick lines in her design. When using line or brush you can choose thicker or thinner lines and brush sizes. Pick the width that is suitable for your needs.

The brush tool

The line tool

Line widths

Brush shapes

WHAT YOU HAVE TO DO

Follow the instructions on this page to create the tree design.

Create a new, original design, suitable for an environmental charity,

Save and print each design and put the print-outs into your IT folder.

2. Mug shots (2)

On this page you will look at more work on the *Mug Shots* project, particularly using the magnify and text options. Follow the instructions on this page to create your own version of the design.

Introduction

On the last page you saw how Alice created a mug design for the charity *Protect Our World*. On this page you will see how she made detailed changes to improve the picture.

You will also see how she added words to the design.

Bitmap

There are several different ways that a computer can create a graphic. One way is for the electronic memory of the computer to store the colour and position of all the pixels. A graphic created in this way is called a **bitmap** graphic.

The Microsoft *Paint* package is a bitmap graphic package.

Pixels

A picture on the computer screen is like a picture on a TV screen. It is made up of millions of little dots. A single one of these dots is called a **pixel**. **Pixel** is short for **PICture ELement**.

When viewed from a distance the eye sees these dots as a whole picture.

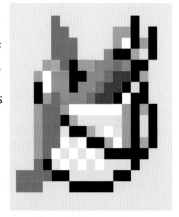

Magnify

By using the **magnify** icon on the tool bar you can look at the pattern of pixels which makes the graphic. On this page you can see how Alice used magnify to make detailed corrections to the image.

Alice had a problem to solve. Because of the way the picture was made there is a thin line halfway up the trunk. She could delete it using the *eraser* but it is a very detailed correction, and she might end up spoiling the picture.

The first thing she did was to **magnify** the image.

● Click on the **magnify** tool to see the picture in close-up detail

The magnify tool

This area will be magnified

After magnification it looks like this.

The pencil tool

The choice of magnification

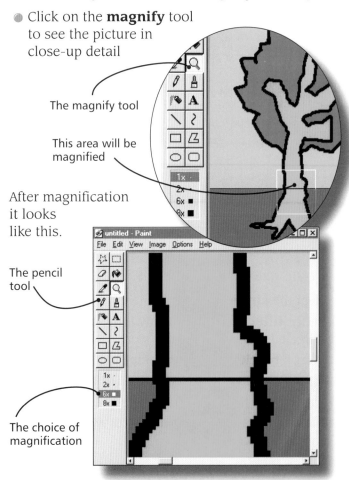

She then used this method to make the correction.

- Select the pencil tool
- Select the light brown colour used for the trunk
- Draw over the thin line

And finally she used this method to return to full size.

- Select the magnification tool again
- Pick the **1×** (times one) magnification to return to normal size

Add text

Alice also wanted to add the words *Protect Our World* to the picture. Again, try to follow these instructions yourself if you can.

- Click on the *colour palette* to pick a colour
- Click on the **text** tool
- Drag on the screen to draw a text box

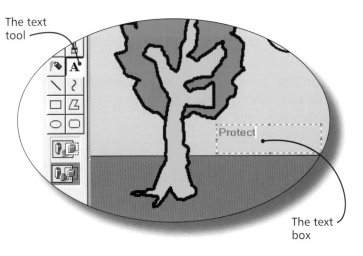

The text tool

The text box

The words you type will appear in the text box.

Be careful when you type in text because if you click with the mouse outside the text box it will disappear, and you won't be able to make any more changes to the words you have typed.

Font

You might want to change the appearance of the text. The style of text is called the **font**. There are lots of fonts available.

There is a text tool bar with all the fonts listed on it. To see this tool bar:

- Open the **View** menu
- Pick **Text Tool** bar

It looks like this.

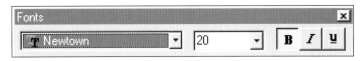

The fonts are stored as *drop down* menus, which you can *scroll* through.

In this example Alice chose a font called *Newtown* and a font size of 20 points. She used brown text on the blue background and blue text on the brown background.

The design is now complete. She saved and printed it.

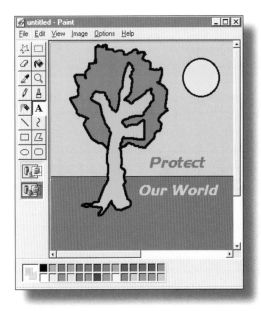

WHAT YOU HAVE TO DO

1. Follow the instructions on this page to modify the design and add text to it. Save and print.

2. Load the second design which you created and add a slogan for your environmental group to it.

Keep your work in your IT folder.

3. Extending the design

On this page you will see how a pupil made changes to her work. You can try out new ideas for yourself, and evaluate the results.

Introduction

The project that the pupils are working on is to create a design for printing on the side of a mug. The design should be in the form of a strip that can be printed around the mug.

On this page you will see how Alice adapted her design to meet these requirements. She tried two different techniques and compared the results.

Page set up

Normally when work is printed from a computer it is produced in *portrait* form. That means the page is set so that it is taller than it is wide.

For the mug design the pupils want to print a page which is wider than it is tall. This is called *landscape*.

Portrait

Landscape

It is easy to change to landscape format.

● Open the **File** menu
● Pick **Page Set̲up...**

You will see a window that lets you pick the style of page you want. On the right is an example of what it might look like. Your computer may be different.

● Simply click on **Landscape** and the **OK** button

Print preview

You might like to check what the graphic will look like when it is printed out. It's a good idea to check before you print. If it looks wrong, then you can change it.

Print preview lets you see what your work will look like.

● Open the **File** menu and pick **Print Pre̲view**

When Alice picked **Print Pre̲view** she saw this on the screen.

You can see how the landscape printing works and that the design looks quite suitable for printing onto a mug.

Trying things out

You often want to try the effect of making changes to your work. You can produce several different versions and then pick the one that you like best.

It is a good idea to save and print your work before you make changes. If you are trying to choose between different versions of the same work, save each version using a different file name. This means that all the versions will be available on your disk.

Remind yourself how to save and how to use different file names, by looking back to page 15.

Copy and paste ■

The first change Alice tried was to put several copies of the tree round the side of the mug. To remind yourself how the clipboard is used to make copies look back to page 16.

First she had to **select** the tree design. With a bitmap package like *Paint* you can't select whole objects. Instead you select an area of the screen. There are two tool bar icons – one lets you select a square area of screen and one lets you select an irregular shape. The tree is an irregular shape.

- Pick the selection tool and draw a line around the tree

The tree is selected

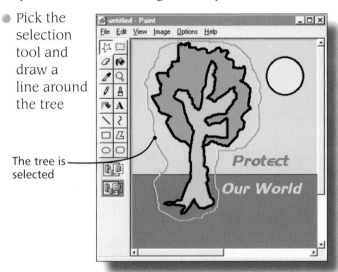

Now that the tree is selected it can be copied onto the clipboard and pasted back into the picture.

- Copy the tree onto the clipboard
- Paste the tree from the clipboard
- Drag the second tree to another part of the picture
- Paste and drag a third tree

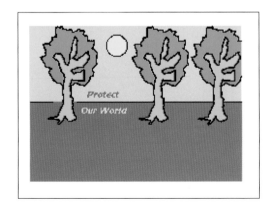

Print preview shows you what the design looks like with three trees.

What do you think about this new design?

Stretch ■

Alice decided to try at least one more effect. Instead of making copies of the tree, she decided to stretch it to cover the whole mug.

- Go back to the original design
- Delete the words and the sun
- Select the tree as before

To stretch the tree you can **drag** the border drawn round the selected area. As you drag the border, the tree is stretched. When Alice did this the tree lost its colour and she had to pour the colour back in again. She added some words in a different font too. It ended up looking like this.

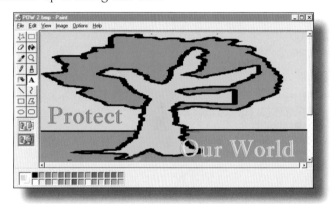

What do you think about this version of the design? Is it an improvement? What would it look like printed round a mug?

The pupils in the class printed out their favourite designs, and stuck the paper round a mug to get an impression of what the designs would look like.

WHAT YOU HAVE TO DO

1. Follow the instructions on this page to produce the two designs shown here. Print each one and save it using a new file name.

2. Produce some different variations on the mug design theme. Try changing colours and other features.

Keep your work in your IT folder.

➡ 31

4. Castle draw

On this page you will look at CorelDRAW. This is a different type of graphics package. You will see how pupils used it to help with a project.

Vector graphics

So far you have looked at the *Paint* type of graphics packages. These are very straightforward packages with a limited range of graphics tools.

Here you will look at a more complex graphics package. You will look at examples of schoolwork produced using this package.

Many advanced graphics packages use **vector** graphics instead of **bitmap** graphics.

If you draw a line in a bitmap package the computer stores the colour and position of all the dots that make the line. If you draw a line in vector graphics the computer stores the start and finish points only, and then draws a line between these two points. All the lines and shapes you draw are stored in a similar way.

This change means that using vector graphics feels quite different from using a bitmap package.

- You can't rub out part of a line or shape; you have to erase the whole line.
- You **select** complete shapes instead of areas of screen.
- You can fill shapes with colour but you can't pour colour into the screen.

Vector packages offer you lots of interesting graphics effects. In this spread and the one that follows you will look at just a few of these.

CorelDRAW is used as an example of a vector graphics package. Don't worry if you don't have this package available at school. Any package with the word *Draw* in the title (plus many others) is likely to be a vector package.

Coreldrw

The project

A class was learning about castles. The pupils investigated how castles were made, and the names of the different features.

They were asked to make a computer graphic relating to this topic. It could be a drawing of a castle, a plan or a diagram. They used a vector package to do this work.

The CorelDRAW window

Here is the window you see when you start **CorelDRAW**. Stephen, one of the pupils, has started to draw a plan of a castle.

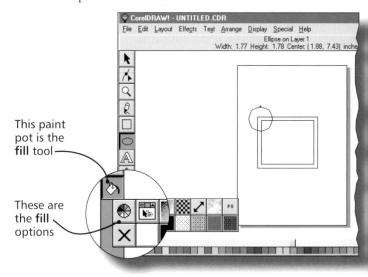

This paint pot is the **fill** tool

These are the **fill** options

To copy this graphic:

- Draw two rectangles, one inside the other
- Draw a circle in one corner

Stephen has clicked on the **fill** tool, and a set of fill options has appeared.

i Put into the clipboard *p17*   Bitmap *p28*

Here is the next stage. The circle has been filled in with white. The pupil has selected the circle by clicking on it with the **arrow** tool.

- Click on plain white to fill the circle

The **arrow** tool lets you select an object

The text tool

The selected object is marked with square **handles**

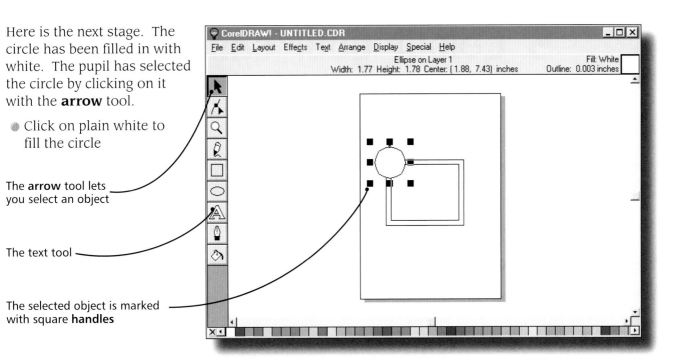

You can now copy, paste and drag the selected object in order to put a circle in each corner of the rectangle. To remind yourself about copy and paste, look on page 16.

- Copy the selected circle to the clipboard
- Drag the selected circle to another corner of the rectangle
- Paste the circle from the clipboard
- Continue to drag and paste until there is a circle in each corner

Stephen also added labels using the text tool.

Here is the completed plan, with added text labels.

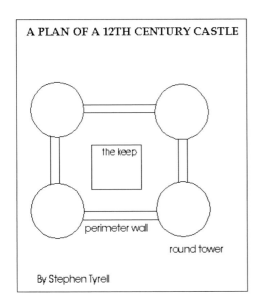

A PLAN OF A 12TH CENTURY CASTLE

the keep

perimeter wall

round tower

By Stephen Tyrell

Here is another diagram of a castle. See if you can copy this using the vector graphics package. To draw freehand use the **pencil** tool and draw with the mouse button held down.

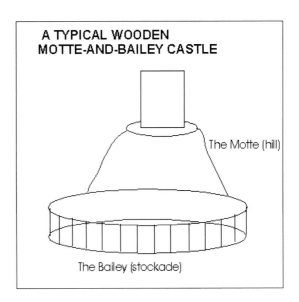

A TYPICAL WOODEN MOTTE-AND-BAILEY CASTLE

The Motte (hill)

The Bailey (stockade)

WHAT YOU HAVE TO DO

Use a vector graphics package, such as CorelDRAW, to create your own version of at least one of the castle pictures on this page.

5. Colour your castle

On this page you will look at one of the most popular features of CorelDRAW – its special colour effects. Have a look at the examples given on this page and then try some effects for yourself.

Special colour effects

CorelDRAW offers some interesting colour effects. On this page you will look at how you can use these to enhance your drawings.

Fill objects

To add colour to a picture you need to fill the objects in your graphic with colour.

As an example let's look at a picture of a castle, and how it can be changed by adding colours and special effects.

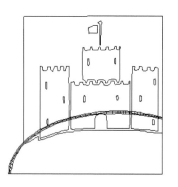

Here is the castle as it was drawn to start with, using outline shapes. Anita, the pupil who drew this, has also drawn a hill for the castle to sit on using the **round shapes** tool.

Adding colours

The colour palette is at the bottom of the screen. You can colour any shape by clicking on it with the selection tool, and then clicking on the colour you want.

Using the colour palette Anita made the castle look like this.

Special effects

As well as plain colours you can fill shapes with **special effects**.

Cloud pattern

- Click on the fill tool to see this choice of effects

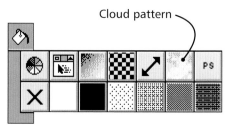

- Click on the cloud pattern for special effects

Vector packages use mathematical formulas to generate complex, natural-looking, colour effects. You can choose the effects you want to use from the next window.

Pick the effect you want   Preview what the effect looks like

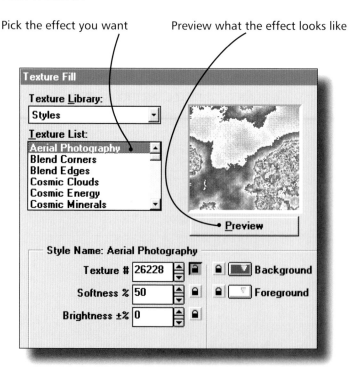

i Making an impression *p23*

Anita selected each object in the castle picture and added special colour effects. This is what it looked like.

The computer mixes together two or more colours to give a natural-looking texture.

Changing the colour effects you use can make the picture look completely different.

You can select several objects at once by holding down the **Shift** key as you click on each.

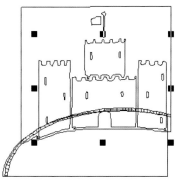

All the parts of the castle have been selected

Select a group of objects

The castle itself in this drawing is made up of several **objects**. You can select the objects one at a time by clicking on each one with the arrow-shaped selection tool.

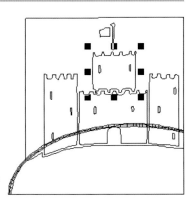

The top tower has been selected

The selected object has been marked with eight square **handles**.

Move and resize

By dragging anywhere on the selected object you can move it to a new place. If you have selected a group of objects they will all move together.

By dragging the handles which mark the edge of the object you can stretch or shrink the object. If you have selected a group of objects they will all shrink or grow together.

Exploring effects

This book does not explain to you how to use all the features of Corel*DRAW*. It does not show you all of the colour effects which are available. Instead you should explore the features for yourself.

If you save your picture to disk or your user area, you can try out different changes and see what happens. If you like the effect of a change you can save the file using a new name. In this way you can build up a selection of files on your disk.

On Target

In this unit you have learned how to create computer graphics. You should know:

- about the different types of computer graphics
- how to create the different types of graphic
- how to vary graphic features to meet your requirements.

WHAT YOU HAVE TO DO

Enhance the castle drawing you created by using colour and special effects. Try out the effects of making changes to colour and other features. Save a selection of your images showing different colours and features.

3 Word Processing

In this unit you will look at word processing software – used to prepare text and all items based mainly around printed words.

On Target

You should already know how to:

- use the keyboard to enter text
- correct the errors in documents
- change the appearance of text features.

In this unit you will revise these skills and learn about:

- combining text files to create large documents
- working with document features and styles
- illustrating documents.

Getting the benefits

You probably still write much of your schoolwork with a pen on paper. People at work used to use a typewriter. Word processing is an alternative to other ways of preparing text.

So what are the main benefits? Why not simply stick to writing all your work with a pen and paper?

Using a word processor offers you several advantages. It can make your work *easier* and it can make your work *better*.

In this introduction will be shown some of the benefits of using a word processor:

- work that looks good
- fewer mistakes
- less effort for you
- the chance to try things out and experiment.

Work that looks good

Some people have very neat handwriting, and some people are not so neat. The printout from a computer is always neat and tidy. When you want your work to look particularly smart, using word processing software can be a good idea.

Another benefit of using the computer is to help with drafting. It's easy to make corrections without untidy crossing out. No matter how many times you have corrected your work it still looks neat and tidy.

But that's not all. By using a word processor you can:

- add effects and improvements to your text to make it look exactly how you like
- make text larger and more colourful
- change the way that words are laid out on the page
- add graphs and pictures to your work.

Do you want some help with gardening?
We are a group of young people looking for part-time work. Hire us to come and work on your garden every week. Or we can help with single tasks like clearing ground and replanting.
If you are interested call
Sally McDonald
01789 - 472985

DO YOU WANT SOME HELP WITH GARDENING?

We are a group of young people looking for part time work. Hire us to come and work on your garden every week. Or we can help with single tasks like clearing ground and replanting.

If you are interested call
Sally McDonald
01789 - 472983

Both these notes give the same information – but which gives a better impression?

Fewer mistakes ■

The computer will find mistakes in your work and help you to correct them.

- A **spell checker** will find spelling mistakes, and suggest the right spelling for you.
- You can print out your work and check it for errors, and then make changes.
- Making changes is easy, and doesn't make a mess of your work.

In all these ways the computer will help you to keep your work free of errors.

The reason why poeple moved to the towns was because there wasn't enough work in the countryside and they wanted to find jobs in the factorys.

You must write more than this. Watch out for spelling mistakes.

You can avoid this kind of problem by using a word processor

Audience ■

In the graphics unit you saw that it was important to think about the **audience** when you create an image (see page 24). The same thing applies when you create a document.

Of course you have to choose your words carefully to suit your audience, and your English teacher can help you to do this. But as well as choosing the right words you should also think about the way you present those words. All the word processing features you learn about in this section will help you to make sure your work suits your audience.

Who is your audience?

IT at work

When householders need a repair or alteration to their house, they usually call a tradesperson, such as a plumber. The plumber will examine the work that needs to be done. If it is not urgent a *quote* or an *estimate* will be provided for the work.

The quote will detail the work that needs to be done, how long it will take, and how much it will cost. Often householders obtain several quotes, before they decide who will do the work.

Nowadays plumbers and other tradespersons frequently use word processing software to prepare their quotes, and other letters that they send to their customers. This is a big change from a few years ago when quotes were typed or handwritten. There are several advantages for the plumber:

- all the quotes given out can be saved as computer files
- quotes have a neat and professional appearance
- it is easy to adapt a quote if circumstances change.

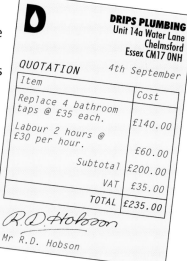

DRIPS PLUMBING
Unit 14a Water Lane
Chelmsford
Essex CM17 0NH

QUOTATION   4th September

Item	Cost
Replace 4 bathroom taps @ £35 each.	£140.00
Labour 2 hours @ £30 per hour.	£60.00
Subtotal	£200.00
VAT	£35.00
TOTAL	£235.00

R.D.Hobson
Mr R.D. Hobson

Less effort ■

There are many ways in which word processing software can save you time and trouble when you are doing schoolwork. Here are some examples.

● Have you ever written a rough version of your work, and then made a neat copy? With word processing you don't need to do your work twice, because the first copy is neat.

● Have you ever needed more than one copy of a piece of work? With word processing you can print out as many copies as you like.

● Have you ever finished your work, and then needed to make a big change to it? With word processing you can make any change you like, and there is no need to rewrite the whole thing.

● Have you had to write the same piece of text over and over again? With word processing you can copy and paste blocks of text, so you only need to type the words once.

So word processing can help you to finish your work more quickly and with less effort. This will help you to get work in *on time*. You might be able to do more in the time available. It also gives you more time to *think about the content* of your work.

Try out and experiment ■

Using word processing software gives you more freedom with your work. It gives you the freedom to try things out, and to experiment.

● Try out different layouts of text. Try out different styles of printing. Try putting different pictures in your work. Which effect looks the best?

● Try using different words. Try organising your work under different headings. Which way is easier to understand?

● Try rearranging the paragraphs or sentences into a new order. Try cutting out sections, or adding new sections. Experiment with different ways of expressing yourself. Which way is most suitable for your needs?

With word processing it is safe to try out something a bit unusual. If it doesn't work out – no harm has been done. Using word processing might encourage you to be more adventurous and make your work more exciting. Or it might help you to make your work more serious and suitable for its purpose.

Three styles of work, which one would you choose? There isn't a right answer – the decision is up to you

History

A lot of the work you do at school in different subjects involves putting words down on paper. Word processing can help with any work of this kind. But it is most useful when:

● you want the presentation of the work to be extremely neat and attractive

● you might need to make changes at the last minute.

A pupil was investigating the Suffragettes, who campaigned to give women the vote in the early 20th century.

The pupil collected together a lot of information and pictures and created an illustrated guide using a word processing package.

The Suffragettes

By Elizabeth Jackson

100 years ago women were not allowed to vote in elections. The 'Suffragettes' were a group of women who campaigned for a change in the law to give the vote to women. Nowadays a group like this is called a 'Pressure Group'.

Drafting

Drafting is a good way to improve your work. This is how you do it:

● Using a word processor, create a first version of the work. This is called the first draft. You don't have to get it right at this stage, just do your best.

● Print out the first draft.

● Read through the first draft, and make corrections and changes. Mark up the printout with a pen to show every correction and change. You might want to show your first draft to someone else, such as your teacher, for comments.

● Load the file again and make all the corrections and changes that you have marked on the printout.

You can continue this process as many times as you like, working with a second or third draft until you are completely happy with your work.

Drafting is a good way to work because it takes away some of the pressure you might feel to get it right first time. You don't have to print out a final version to hand in until you are completely happy with what you have done.

WHAT YOU HAVE TO DO

Four pupils have four different problems. How could using a word processor help each of these pupils? Write a short piece of advice for each pupil.

1. Natalie works with great care, but she often hands in work late, or unfinished.

2. Sean's handwriting is very untidy.

3. Mohammed has good ideas, but his spelling is terrible.

4. Emily notices errors after she has finished her work. She doesn't want to mess it up with lots of corrections and crossing out.

Keep your work in your IT folder.

I. Getting a plum job

On this page you will look at how pupils used a word processor to help them prepare text for a newspaper project.

Preparing text

On this page you can see what work you can do with a word processor. You can look at how a pupil used word processing to:

- prepare text
- correct errors
- organise a document
- make his work look better.

Start up a word processing package and try to do the same work that you see on this page.

Microsoft *Word*

Microsoft Word

The word processing package used as an example in this section is called **Microsoft *Word***. There are several different versions of Word and there are several different word processing packages.

However, they all work in much the same way, so you should be able to follow the work, no matter what package you use at school.

The project

In this unit you will look at how a class worked together to create a class newspaper of real life stories.

Everyone in the class had to find a story from a newspaper. Many pupils were able to bring in old newspapers from home, and the teacher provided some too. They looked through the newspapers for short funny stories. Then they typed them up, either copying the words from the newspaper, or using their own words.

One pupil, Jack Horner, found an interesting story about plum jam. Here you will see how he used a word processing package to type it up ready for the newspaper.

The story

This is what the story looked like the first time the pupil typed it up.

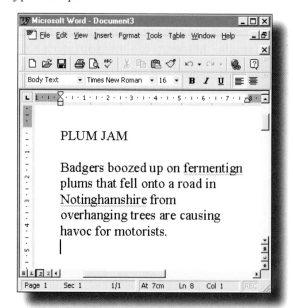

Either copy this work, or find a similar short amusing story and type it up using word processing software.

Spelling

There are two careless spelling mistakes in the story. The word processing package has spotted them and marked them with a wiggly red line.

To correct the mistakes:

● Click on the word with the right mouse button

You will see a spelling menu, which looks something like this:

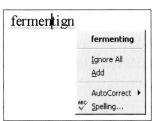

The computer has suggested the right spelling. Sometimes it has several suggestions and you have to pick the right one.

Sometimes the computer doesn't recognise a word even though it is spelled correctly. If you are sure a spelling is right you can click on **Ignore All** and the computer will ignore that word when checking for spellings. You can even click on **Add** and the computer will add the word to the list of words it knows.

● Click on the correct spelling from the menu

Moving text

It is very easy to move a block of text from one place to another on the screen.

● Select the block you want to move

Remember that you select a block of text by dragging the mouse pointer over the text, with the mouse button held down.

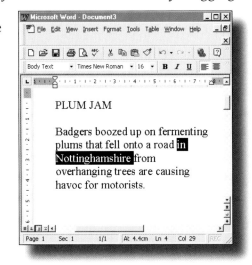

The selected text is highlighted

Next you can move the text.

● Click anywhere in the highlighted block and drag it to the new position

Formatting text

Finally Jack decided to **format** the *headline* of his story. Formatting means changing the appearance of the text. He decided to make the headline bigger, bolder and more colourful than the rest of the text.

Many different formatting options are available on the tool bar. You can click on formatting tools before you type text, or you can select the text and then format it.

● Select the text you want to format

The text can be formatted as **bold**.

The **size** of the text can be changed.

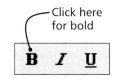

Click here for bold

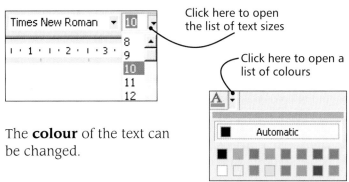

Click here to open the list of text sizes

Click here to open a list of colours

The **colour** of the text can be changed.

● Experiment with different formats, and format the headline of your story

Here is what the story looked like when all the changes had been made.

Do you think this is an improvement on the original version? Would you prefer the headline to be black or red, or some other colour?

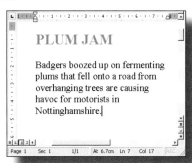

WHAT YOU HAVE TO DO

1. **Copy the work shown on this page, formatting the text in whatever style you want.**

2. **Find a different short newspaper story, and type it up in a similar style.**

Remember to save and print all your work, and put it in your IT folder.

2. A Bizarre story

On this page you will see how you can combine several short documents to make one large document.

Combining documents

All the pupils in a class typed up short items they had collected from newspapers. Here you will see how the different stories were copied into one large document – making a class newspaper.

If you can, work through this page with some other people from your class. If you have each prepared a different story, combine them to make a single large document.

Preparation ▪

Before they started, the pupils copied all the different files into one storage location. To remind yourself about copying and moving files between storage locations, look on page 21.

- Decide on a storage location (a disk or a directory)
- Copy your file into this location (everyone in the group should do this)
- Start up the graphics package and open all the files

The graphics packages you used will only open one file at a time. But *Word*, and many other Windows packages, will allow you to open several files at once. This means you can easily copy pieces of work from one document to another.

- Open each file, one after the other.
- Start a new, blank, document
- Save this empty document using a suitable file name (like *newspaper*)

Swap between files ▪

If you open the **Window** menu of the word processing package you will see a list of all the open files.

Window Help
New Window
Arrange All
Split
1 Arpal's article.doc
2 Bob's article.doc
3 Jasmine's article.doc
4 Ladonna's article.doc
5 Roger's article.doc
6 Soo Li's article.doc
✓ 7 THE NEWSPAPER.doc

Whichever file you click on will be displayed in the working area of the word processing package.

You can use this menu to quickly swap between the different files that are open.

Copy text ▪

- Use the **Window** menu to select one of the stories
- Select all the text in the story
- Copy the text onto the clipboard

To remind yourself how to use the clipboard, look on page 16.

- Use the **Window** menu to select the empty newspaper document
- Paste the text from the clipboard

Repeat these stages until all the stories are copied into one document.

The newspaper

This is what the newspaper looked like when the stories had all been copied together. The class got together to discuss what they thought of it.

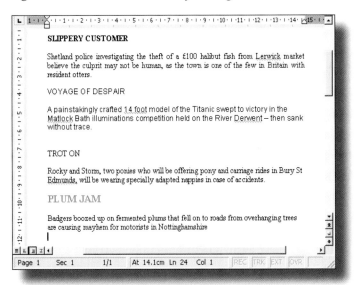

What's wrong with this document?

The pupils decided that the newspaper didn't look too good, because they each used a different style for their stories. They needed to adjust the format.

When you combine different documents together you have to check that features like text style and colour are the same all the way through.

- Check the formats used in the different articles
- If necessary change format style to make it the same all the way through

Next the pupils discussed what to call the newspaper. They decided on *Bizarre News*.

They worked together to write a short introduction, called an *editorial*, and typed it up. They had to work out what to do about **justification** and **columns**.

Justification

Justification means how text is arranged on the page. Look at a real newspaper. You will probably see that the title is **centred** (in the centre of the page) and the main text is **fully justified** (with straight margins on both sides of the page).

Select the text you want to format and use tool bar icons to pick a suitable layout.

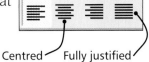

Centred   Fully justified

Columns

The other feature you might have noticed when you were looking at newspapers is that text is often arranged into columns.

- Select all the text except the title and editorial
- Click on this tool bar icon to organise it into columns

The columns tool

Be careful not to have too many columns. Very short lines of text are difficult to read.

The result

This is what the finished document looked like.

BIZARRE NEWS

News stories collected by Communications group 5
Week ending 5/5/99

EDITORIAL

Welcome to 'Bizarre News' a free newspaper from Communications group 5. In it you will read news stories that we found amusing.

SLIPPERY CUSTOMER

Shetland police investigating the theft of a £100 halibut fish from Lerwick market believe the culprit may not be human, as the town is one of the few in Britain with resident otters.

VOYAGE OF DESPAIR

A painstakingly crafted 14 foot model of the titanic swept to victory in the Matlock Bath illuminations competition held on the River Derwent – then sank without trace.

TROT ON

Rocky and Storm, two ponies who will be offering pony and carriage rides in Bury St Edmunds, will be wearing specially adapted nappies in case of accidents.

PLUM JAM

Badgers boozed up on fermented plums that fell on to roads from overhanging trees are causing mayhem for motorists in Nottinghamshire

WHAT YOU HAVE TO DO

Get together with some other pupils who have also typed up newspaper stories. Copy all your different stories into one large file. Adjust formats and add a title and introduction.

Print out enough copies of the newspaper to have one each. Put your copy in your IT folder.

3. Using clip art

Next you will learn how to add pictures and other graphics to your documents to make them more interesting.

Illustrating a document (1)

You have seen how a class created a newspaper using word processing software. On this page you will see how they added pictures to the newspaper. They used three types of **illustration**:

- the clip art provided with the word processing package
- graphics from a commercial source
- graphics that they had created themselves.

Here you will look at using clip art. Other options are covered on the next spread.

Find clip art

The easiest way to add graphics to the document is to use the clip art provided free with the word processing package. To find a suitable picture among this selection:

- Open the **Insert** menu
- Pick **Picture** from the Insert menu
- Pick **Clip Art...** from the second menu that appears

When you open **Clip Art** you will see this window.

The pictures are organised into categories. You can look through all the pictures to find the one you want. Or you can search using keywords. Every picture in the clip art gallery is described in words. You can enter a keyword and the computer will find all the pictures that match that word.

- Click on the **Find** button

Find Now

You will see the *Find Clip* screen.

- Enter one or more keywords
- Click on the **Find Now** button

The keyword – the pupils have entered the word *news*

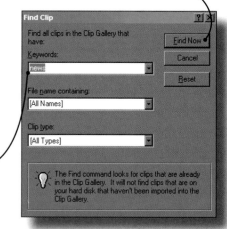

Here are the pictures that the computer found for them.

Categories

Pictures within a category

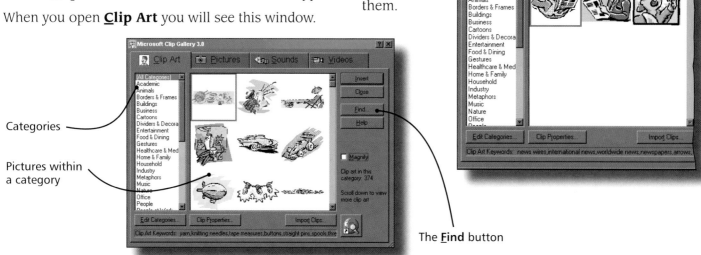

The **Find** button

Move and resize graphics ▪

You can select any picture in the document.

● Click on the picture

The edge of the graphic will be marked with eight little squares called **resize handles**.

● Click and drag anywhere inside the area marked by handles to move the picture to a new place

● Click and drag the handles to change the size of the picture

Resize handles

If you drag the corner handles the picture will change size but *stay the same* shape.

If you drag the other handles the picture will change shape *as well as* size.

You need to make sure the picture is in the right place, and is the right size and shape.

More Bizarre News ▪

The class chose this clip art image to go at the top of the newspaper. It doesn't illustrate a particular story, but it shows that the document is a newspaper.

● Is this the image you would have chosen?

● Where would you place it in the newspaper?

On the next page you will see some more ideas about illustrating the document.

Wrapping

When you first insert a picture into a piece of text the words probably stop above and below the picture.

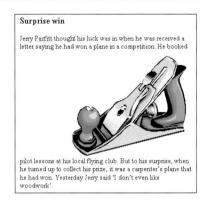

Surprise win

Jerry Parfitt thought his luck was in when he was received a letter saying he had won a plane in a competition. He booked

pilot lessons at his local flying club. But to his surprise, when he turned up to collect his prize, it was a carpenter's plane that he had won. Yesterday Jerry said 'I don't even like woodwork'.

But you can make the text 'wrap' around the picture. Here is how to do it.

● Right click on the picture – a menu appears

● Pick **Format Picture** from the menu

You will see a window with labelled 'tabs' along the top.

The *Wrapping* tab

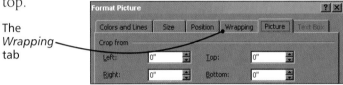

● Click on the tab that says **Wrapping**

In this window you can pick the type of wrapping you want. Experiment with different styles if you have time.

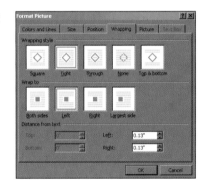

WHAT YOU HAVE TO DO

Make sure you have a copy of the newspaper file.

1. **Look through the clip art provided with your word processing package. Find at least one clip art image which is suitable for the newspaper.**

2. **Insert this clip art into the newspaper.**

3. **Position and size the image to make a suitable illustration for the newspaper.**

Save and print the illustrated newspaper.

Keep your work in your IT folder.

4. It's in the picture

On this page you will look at other sources of illustrations, and how to choose the right pictures for your needs.

Illustrating a document (2)

When you choose a picture you need to think about why you want to put a picture into your document.

- To make it look more inviting?
- To produce some other kind of impact on the reader?
- To illustrate a particular point?
- To provide specific information?

When you look through a clip art collection, make sure you keep the above questions in mind.

If your picture has to illustrate a particular point, or provide specific information, then make sure you know exactly:

- what the subject of the picture must be
- what details it must include.

If you can't find the picture that does the job you want it to then you will have to make it yourself using a computer graphics package.

When you are choosing or designing graphics to go into your documents, remember to think about the **audience** for your work. Always ask yourself who will look at your document, and try to imagine what they will think of your pictures. Look back to page 24 for more information about graphics and audiences.

Using commercial clip art

As well as clip art provided with the word processing package, you can buy sets of clip art. Clip art is usually provided on a set of CDs. The CDs may hold tens of thousands of pictures. They may include photos as well as drawings. Your school may have such a package available in a resource room for you to access.

The different commercial clip art packages provide different types of *interface* to let you look through and find the picture you want. Here is one example.

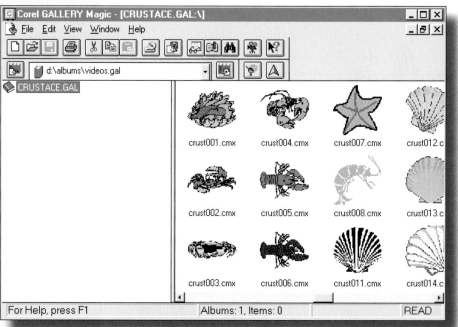

It is worth finding out how to use the clip art resources at your school because it makes lots of pictures available to you.

i Create graphics p26

Photos

You might also have the chance to use commercial photos. Photos take up more disk space so there may be a smaller selection to look through. Below is one package which lets you pick photos to put into your documents.

Investigate whether photos are available on the computer system at your school.

Make your own graphics

You can make your own graphics using a suitable package. Then copy them into your document using the clipboard. Look on page 16 to remind yourself how to do this.

Modern word processing packages often have a vector graphics feature, which you can use to draw graphics straight into the document.

● Click on this icon on the tool bar to see the graphics feature

A bar with graphics tools appears. Use them to draw lines and shapes straight into your document.

If you know how, you could also create your own photographs using a digital camera, or by scanning in pictures.

The final result

Here is what the newspaper looked like with pictures added to it. What do you think of it?

BIZARRE NEWS

News stories collected by Communications group 5
Week ending 5/5/99

EDITORIAL

Welcome to 'Bizarre News' a free newspaper from Communications group 5. In it you will read news stories that we found amusing.

SLIPPERY CUSTOMER

Shetland police investigating the theft of a £100 halibut fish from Lerwick market believe the culprit may not be human, as the town is one of the few in Britain with resident otters.

VOYAGE OF DESPAIR

A painstakingly crafted 14 foot model of the titanic swept to victory in the Matlock Bath illuminations competition held on the River Derwent – then sank without trace.

TROT ON

Rocky and Storm, two ponies who will be offering pony and carriage rides in Bury St Edmunds, will be wearing specially adapted nappies in case of accidents.

PLUM JAM

Badgers boozed up on fermented plums that fell on to roads from overhanging trees are causing mayhem for motorists in Nottinghamshire.

WHAT YOU HAVE TO DO

Investigate the other sources of illustrations that are available at your school.

Improve the newspaper still further by adding as many of the following as possible:

■ **commercial clip art**

■ **photos**

■ **graphics you have created yourself.**

5. Take a break

Finally in this unit you will look at how to work with documents that are several pages long.

Working with long documents

The newspaper that the pupils made was several pages long by the time they had finished. On this page you will see some of the features that are available to help you to work with long documents, and how the class used these features.

Scrolling

When a document gets long you can't see it all on the screen at once. Remember you can use the scroll bar to look through a document.

Page setup

On page 30 you saw how to swap between *portrait* and *landscape* pages. Remember you have this choice with text documents as well as graphics files. Sometimes you want a document to be wider than it is tall.

This is what the newspaper looks like in landscape format.

Do you think it looks better like this?

Which format would you choose – portrait or landscape?

Page break

When the document is big enough the computer will automatically start a new page. The page break will be shown on the screen, perhaps as a dotted line.

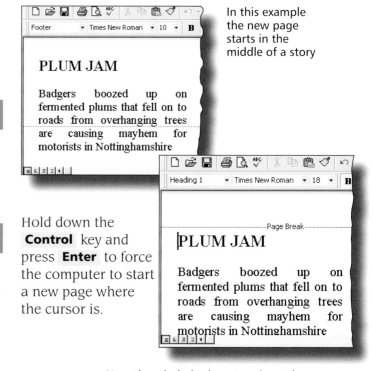

In this example the new page starts in the middle of a story

Hold down the **Control** key and press **Enter** to force the computer to start a new page where the cursor is.

Now the whole *badger* story is on the same page

Page numbers

The pupils wanted to number the pages of their newspaper. You can do this with any of your documents.

● Open the **Insert** menu
● Pick **Page Numbers...**

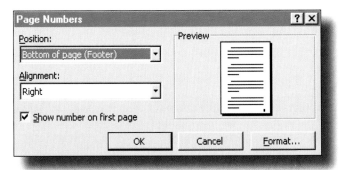

You will see a window like this.

You can use this window to pick the position of the page number. Click **OK** when you have picked the right location. Remember you can use *print preview* to check the appearance of the document before you print it out.

Viewing

Many packages let you change the way you see the document. Instead of seeing part of it in close detail you can have a broader view.

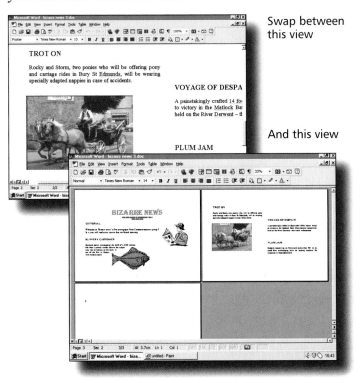

Swap between this view

And this view

To swap between the two views:

● Open the **View** menu
● Pick **Zoom...**

This window lets you choose which type of view you want

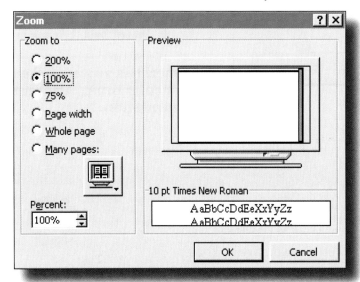

On Target

In this unit you have learned how to create text documents. You should now know how to:

■ create text documents that are suitable for your needs
■ adjust the formatting and layout of documents
■ handle large and small documents
■ create illustrated documents.

WHAT YOU HAVE TO DO

Carry out some more work on the newspaper file.

1. Check for page breaks, and insert new breaks if necessary to stop any of the stories from being split between pages.

2. Add page numbers to the newspaper you created.

3. Print out two versions of the newspaper – one in landscape format and one in portrait format. Which is better?

4 Presentation

Sometimes you are asked to give a presentation on a particular topic. Computers can help you to give a good presentation.

On Target

You should already know:

- how to combine words and pictures
- about sound and video clips
- that software can be used to put together an on-screen presentation.

In this unit you will revise these skills and learn how to:

- plan and structure a presentation
- use computer features to enhance the presentation
- select the design and content of the presentation to make it effective
- give the presentation to your group.

Prepare and present

The first stage is to prepare the visual materials that will support your presentation. Then you use these materials as you give the presentation. Presentation software will help with both of these stages.

By using the software you can:

- put together multimedia materials. You usually make a series of *slides*. Each slide is a computer screen displaying a few words, perhaps a picture too, and other items
- run a presentation where each slide is displayed one after the other on a screen as you give the talk that goes with the slides.

Planning

The key to giving a good presentation is to plan it carefully.

- Make sure you know exactly what you want to communicate.
- Be clear about who your audience is.
- Don't try to communicate too much.
- Say what you mean as clearly and simply as you can.

Sometimes the most important task is deciding what *not* to say

 i Creating slides *p56* Giving the presentation *p62*

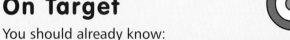

Visual aids ■

There is a difference between an ordinary talk and a presentation. When you give a presentation you have **visual aids** to help you. Visual aids are things that people can look at while you give the presentation.

The two good reasons for including visual aids in a presentation are:

- that it is the best way to communicate some information
- because it makes the presentation more interesting and lively.

Here are some visual aids you should not use:

- a display showing a lot of words that you read out
- a display cluttered up with information
- a display which has nothing to do with what you are saying.

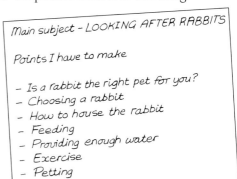

Make your point ■

When you have chosen (or been given) the topic for your presentation, try answering the following questions.

- What is the main message of my presentation?
- How can I split that up into points?
- In what order should I present the points?

The answers to these questions will give you the structure of your presentation.

Each display in the presentation should make one point. The point should be clear to you. You must pick a visual aid, and words to speak, that will make the point clear to the audience. If your presentation has more than 10–15 points then it is too long.

Here is a plan that a pupil made for a presentation about caring for rabbits.

Main subject – LOOKING AFTER RABBITS

Points I have to make

– Is a rabbit the right pet for you?
– Choosing a rabbit
– How to house the rabbit
– Feeding
– Providing enough water
– Exercise
– Petting
– Illnesses

Getting IT Right in...

English

Giving a presentation is a way of showing what you know about a particular subject. Some pupils prefer talking about their interests, rather than writing them down.

A pupil was struggling in English because she wasn't confident as a writer. The teacher found out that this girl was good at looking after rabbits and knew a lot about them.

The teacher asked her to give a presentation about rabbits instead of writing an essay. She was able to talk about rabbits to the whole class, with computer slides to display pictures and a few words. Her presentation was a good way to show her abilities.

LOOKING AFTER RABBITS

By Emma Delaney

Conclusions

- A rabbit is a lot of fun
- Don't buy a rabbit unless you can look after it properly
- Find out what a rabbit needs before you get one

The first and last screens in a presentation about looking after rabbits

A beginning, middle and end ■

Every presentation has a beginning, a middle and an end.

Have you heard that said?

You have decided on a series of points, in order. First, however, your presentation needs an introduction, where you explain what it is about.

At the end, it should finish with a conclusion, where you emphasise the main message of the presentation.

Here are some more wise words about presentations:

Let them know what you are going to tell them,
Tell them,
Remind them of what you have told them,
Do this and you won't go wrong!

Plan your words

Plan what you are going to say as you show each slide in your presentation. Write the words down if you like. Hold your notes as you speak. But try not to read out the words. Speak naturally.

Practise and time

Run through your presentation on your own. Practice it as many times as you like. Practice it in front of members
of your family. They can listen to your words even if they can't see the presentation slides.

Time yourself. Does it take longer than you thought? Or shorter? Will you have to change the amount you want to say?

Confidence

Everyone feels nervous about speaking to a room full of people. Be prepared – know exactly what you are going to say.

If something goes wrong – don't panic. It seems worse to you than your audience. Correct the mistake and carry on.

Designed to please ■

With the right software package it is easy to make big changes to the appearance of a presentation. You have lots of choice about the design you use. Carefully pick a design that will appeal to your audience and produce a good impression.

Imagine you want to encourage people to take good care of their teeth. Here are three ways of getting the same message across.

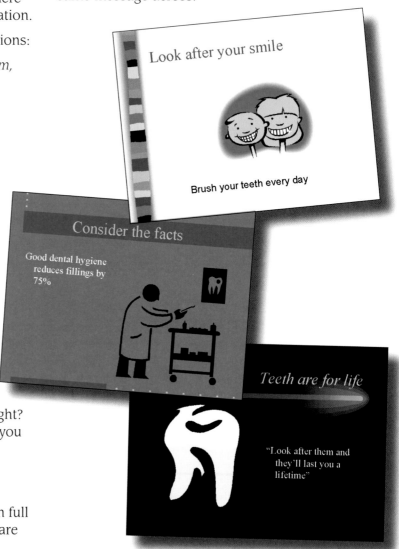

Now answer these questions.

● What might be the target audience for each of these three presentations?

● How have different colours, shapes, pictures and typefaces been used to make each presentation suitable for its audience?

● Have you any suggestions for improvements to any of them?

IT at work

A sports equipment company wanted to advertise a new type of trainer. They gave the contract to an advertising agency.

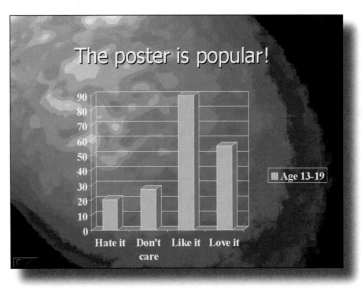

The poster is popular!

The agency came up with ideas for a poster campaign. They designed a set of posters. But they didn't go right ahead with printing up the posters and sticking them up all over the country.

First they had to give a presentation to the sports equipment company. They had to show that the posters were good enough. In the presentation they displayed the posters they had designed. They also displayed graphs showing that 75% of teenagers liked the posters.

Getting organised

An important part of giving a presentation is making sure that the room is organised properly. Make sure that everyone is sitting so that they can see and hear your presentation.

Where do you stand?

Don't hover over the computer screen while you give the presentation.

Stand to one side of the screen, looking straight at your audience. You should know what is on the screen; you don't need to look at it all the time.

Hold the mouse in your hand so you can click to bring up a new screen. When you click to a new screen, glance over to make sure it has come up properly, then turn back to your audience.

PRESENTATION 10.30am

WHAT YOU HAVE TO DO

Megan Pritchard has been asked to give a talk to a group of young children at a local primary school. The children are aged 5 and 6. She has to talk to them about road safety.

Answer these questions for Megan.

1. What is the main message she must communicate?

2. List some of the points she needs to make in the presentation.

I. Doing it with style

On this page you will see how to use the Microsoft *PowerPoint* package to choose the style and colours for a presentation.

Picking a style

PowerPoint

The presentation package used as an example in this book is **Microsoft PowerPoint**. This is a very well known presentation package, though there are others. There are also different versions of *PowerPoint*, with some variations between them.

Microsoft PowerPoint

You should be able to follow the work in this unit whatever package you are using.

The project

A class was studying extinct animals. In this topic they learned about:

- extinct animals such as dinosaurs and mammoths

- how palaeontologists find out about extinct animals

- how animals are still becoming extinct in the present day.

They visited a museum and did several pieces of written work. Then, at the end of term, each pupil was asked to give a short presentation about the topic.

You will see how they did this work, using the computer. Try to follow the work on this page, and the pages that follow. You can copy the presentations shown here, or make up your own work on a topic you and your teacher choose.

Start work

On the last page you saw how you have to plan a presentation carefully, and think about the points you want to make. The next stage is to start making slides.

When you start up *PowerPoint* you may see a window like this.

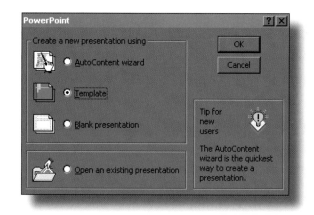

- Pick the **Template** option.

This option gives you a style for the presentation, but not any words. This is the screen you will see next.

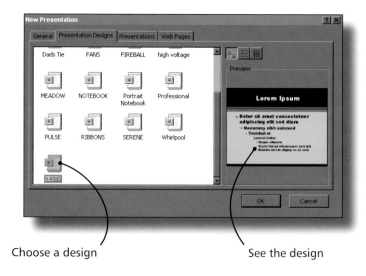

Choose a design   See the design

i Planning p50

Using the **template** option gives you a number of presentation designs that are ready for you to use.

- Click on a design, and see what it looks like
- Pick the design you want to use
- Click on OK

You can change the design later if you like.

The Age of Dinosaurs

Kulvinder Singh

Different styles

The style you choose can make your presentation look quite different.

Kulvinder Singh was one of the pupils who had to give a presentation about extinct animals. He chose the dinosaurs. He tried out three different styles. Using the **template** option he was able to pick a style in just a few seconds. On the right you can see the three different possible styles he created for his presentation.

The Age of Dinosaurs

Kulvinder Singh

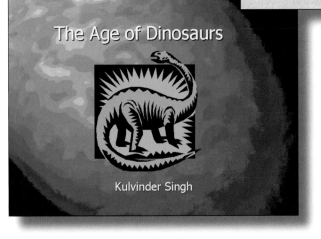

The Age of Dinosaurs

Kulvinder Singh

- Which style do you like best?
- Do you think another of the available styles would be better?

There is no right answer. It is a matter of taste, and depends on the effect you want to produce to meet the needs of your audience.

On the next page you will see how to make presentation slides using the chosen template. If you have time, go straight on to the next page.

If you don't have any more time, note down the template you picked. Next lesson you can start again, by picking this template.

WHAT YOU HAVE TO DO

With your teacher, decide on a suitable topic for a presentation. It could be a personal interest of your own, or it could be a topic taken from one of your school subjects. If you can't think of anything else, pick *Extinct Animals* as shown on this page, or *Road Safety for Kids*.

Away from the computer

1. Note down:

    - the subject of the presentation
    - the main points you want to make.

2. Who is the audience for the presentation?

At the computer

1. Start up a presentation package.

2. Look through the templates and pick the one you like best.

2. Changing slides

On this page you will learn how to make presentation slides, including text and pictures.

Creating slides

On the last page you saw how pupils started to use *PowerPoint* and chose a style for their presentation. Now you will see how pupils created *PowerPoint* **slides**. The slides included words and pictures.

Try to follow the work on this page using the presentation software that is available to you at school.

Remember, you should have started the package, and chosen a presentation design. Look back to the previous page if you need a reminder about how to do this.

Slide = point

You planned a presentation. You set out the points you want to make. Now you should create one slide for each point, plus an introduction and a conclusion.

You can create the slides in any order.

- Pick one point from your list
- Think about how you will illustrate this point with words and pictures

Remember your slide doesn't have to include everything about your point. You probably just want to describe a key point, and include an image to illustrate it.

Choose a layout

The presentation package lets you choose the layout for your slide. After you pick a presentation design, you will see this window.

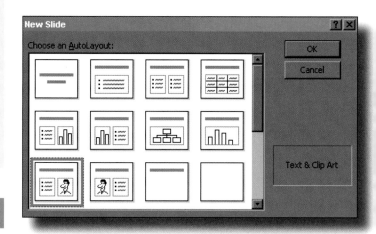

Does the slide you have planned include words only? Words and a picture? A table?

- Pick the layout style for your first slide

You can change the layout later if you want.

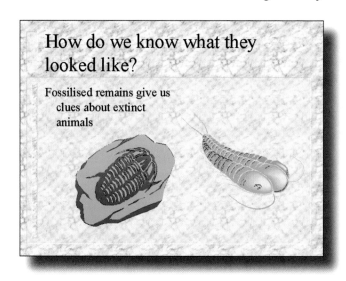

How do we know what they looked like?

Fossilised remains give us clues about extinct animals

i Find clip art *p44* How the clipboard helps *p17*

Empty layout

After you pick a layout you will see an empty slide, something like this, depending on your earlier choices.

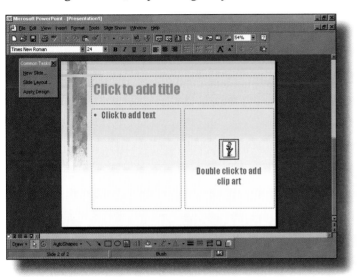

Add words and pictures

The layout gives you space to add the words that go in your slide.

● Click on the text or title boxes
● Type the text you want to show on the slide

Use the word processing features that you have already learned to check and format the text.

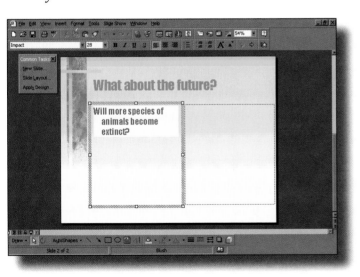

Next you want to add a picture to the slide.

● Select the **picture** section of the layout.
● Double-click to see the clip art selection
● Look through to find a suitable picture
● Click to select it
● Click on the **Insert** key

Other pictures

You are not limited to the clip art provided. Create your own graphics, or take graphics from other sources.

Use **cut** and **paste** to copy pictures into the slide.

Print and save

You can print and save your presentation, just like any other work you do.

WHAT YOU HAVE TO DO

1. **Create one slide for the presentation on your chosen subject.**

2. **Save and print.**

Put your work in your IT folder.

3. Next slide, please!

On this page you will see how you can put together a selection of slides, creating a complete presentation.

Building up the presentation

You have seen how to pick a style. You have seen how to create a single slide, with words and pictures.

Adding another slide

When you create a slide you will see there is a box with three **common tasks** on display next to the slide.

Use this little toolbox to make a new slide.

● Click on the **New Slide...** option in the toolbox

You will see the **layout** window. With this you can pick a layout for the new slide.

Changing the design and layout

The box of common tasks contains two other options.

● Click on **Slide Layout...** to pick a new layout for the current slide

● Click on **Apply Design...** to choose a new style for the entire slideshow

Remember to try out a few design styles. It only takes a second to make the change. You might find one that you like better.

Keep the text and picture the same but vary the design of the screen. Try to find the effect that works best

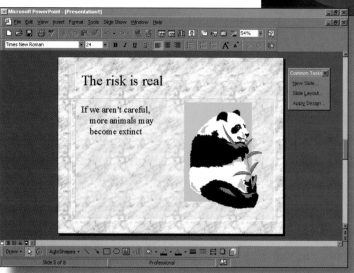

i Different styles p55

Reorganise the slides

Eventually you will build up a complete set of slides for your presentation. You may have created them in any order. It is easy to reorganise them into the right order for the final presentation.

- Open the **View** menu
- Pick **Sli_de Sorter**

Every slide you have created is shown on the screen at once. You can reorganise the slides on this screen.

- Click on a slide you want to move
- Drag it to its new location

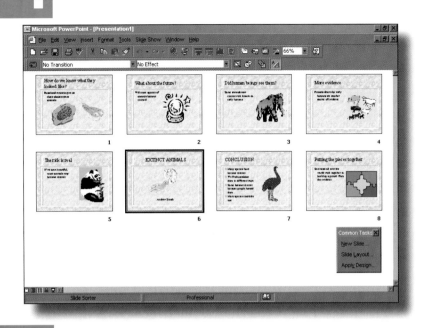

Preview the presentation

You can run through the presentation on the screen of the computer.

- Open the **View** menu
- Select **Slide Sho_w**

Slide 1 of the presentation will be displayed on the screen.

- Press the **Enter** key or the mouse button to move on to the next slide
- On the final screen, press **Enter** to finish the presentation

You can stop at any time.

- Press the **Escape** key to stop the slideshow

You can run through the entire presentation.

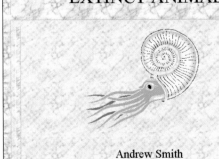

WHAT YOU HAVE TO DO

1. Complete the presentation you are making, by creating all the slides.
2. Rearrange the slides into the right order.
3. Preview the presentation on the screen of your computer.

4. See me, hear me

On this page you will learn how to add sounds and moving images to your presentations.

Sound and video

You can improve your presentations even more by adding **sounds** and **moving images** to them. Here you will see how to do this, and look at how Simon found suitable clips to add to his presentation.

The clip art you get with *PowerPoint* includes animated pictures and sounds. You can insert these clips into presentations.

Edit a slide

You can scroll through your presentation and make changes to slides at any time. Just bring the slide up on the screen and click on the part you want to change.

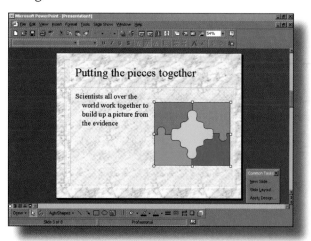

- To change the picture for new clip art, double-click on the picture

- To add extra clip art, click on the clip art button on the tool bar

The clip art window comes up again.

Add a video clip

Video clips are stored in the clip art gallery.

The available video clips   The video tab

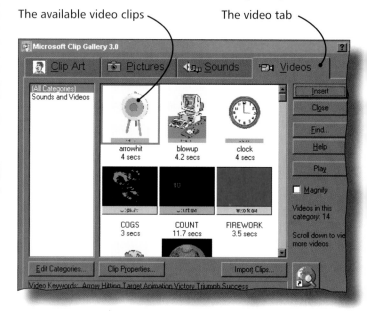

- Click on the **Videos** tab at the top of the window
- Look through the clips which are shown
- Click on the **Play** button to preview the action

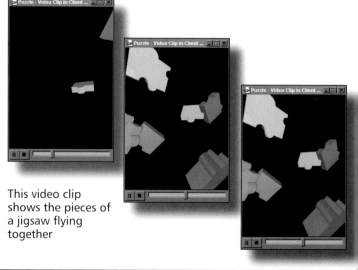

This video clip shows the pieces of a jigsaw flying together

Simon thought that a video of jigsaw pieces would be more interesting than a picture of a jigsaw. Do you agree?

- Click on **Insert** to put the video into the presentation

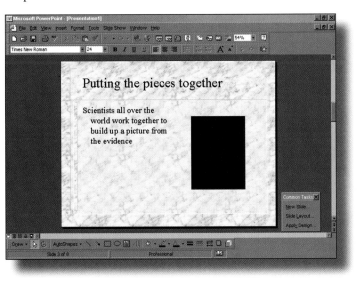

Doesn't look too exciting does it? But when you run the presentation the video will play in the black rectangle.

Add sound

You can also use the clip art window to choose and insert sound clips. The pupil decided to add a sound at the very start of his presentation – to attract everyone's attention when he was ready to start.

- Display the screen that you want to change
- Bring back the clip art window
- Click on the **Sounds** tab

The sound clips   The **Sounds** tab

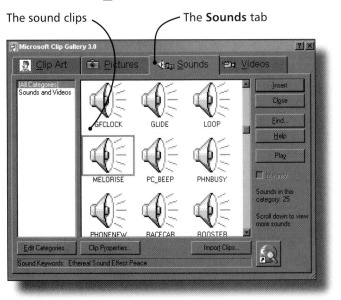

- Select any of the sounds
- Click on **Play** to hear the sound
- When you find a sound you like, click on **Insert**

The screen where the sound has been inserted looks like this.

This little symbol stands for the sound

Again, it's not very exciting to look at. But when you run the presentation the sound will play.

See how to run the presentation, including sound and video, on the next page.

Other sources

If you have other sound or video clips on the computer, then you can include them in your presentation. Use the **Insert** menu, and pick the **Movies and Sounds** option.

When you learn how to use the Internet and to search through CD-ROMs for information you will find samples of video and sound.

WHAT YOU HAVE TO DO

Adapt your presentation by adding at least one sound or video clip.

5. Play it again

Finally in this unit you will see how to give the presentation using the visual aids you have prepared.

Giving the presentation

The pupils prepared a presentation each. Then the time came to give the presentations. Each pupil used the *PowerPoint* file they had created.

Look back to page 55 to remind yourself about organising yourself and the presentation.

Controlling the presentation

To start the *PowerPoint* presentation

- make sure the file is opened and ready
- click **View Slide Show** – this is on the View menu and the **Slide Show** menu.

The first slide in your presentation will fill the whole computer screen. Your mouse pointer will also be on the screen.

The first slide of the presentation

- Click the mouse button to go on to the next slide

If you click too soon, or click twice and miss out a slide, you can use the **Up** and **Down** arrows on the keyboard to go backwards and forwards through the slides.

Play sound and video

- Move the mouse pointer to click on the sound symbol to play the sound
- Click on the animated area to play the animation

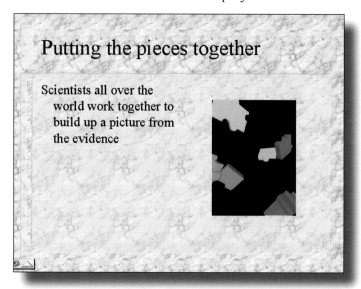

This screen shows the animation running

Slide transition

As you give the presentation you click the mouse button, and a new slide appears. The transition between the two slides is very plain. One disappears and another one takes its place on the screen.

In this section you will learn how to introduce special transition effects, for example a slow fade-out from one slide to another. This is a fun way to make your presentation more personalised and interesting.

- Open the **Slide Show** menu
- Pick **Slide Transition**

You will see this window.

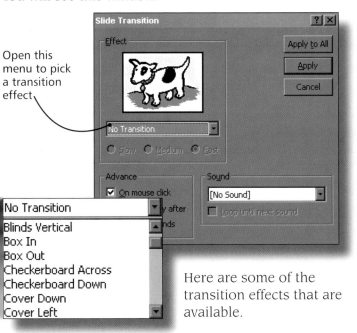

Open this menu to pick a transition effect.

Here are some of the transition effects that are available.

The names shown here give you some idea of what the transition looks like. But you can also see it for yourself. When you select a transition the picture of a dog will turn into a picture of a key, demonstrating the transition.

Customise the transition

If you look at the transition window you will see there are other decisions you can make.

You can make the transition from one slide to another slower or faster.

You can add a sound, which will play when the transition occurs.

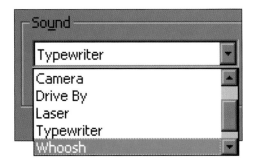

Apply the transition

Once you have picked a suitable transition then you can apply it to the whole presentation, or to the current slide only.

Unless there is a good reason, it is probably best to pick one kind of slide transition, and use it throughout your whole presentation. Otherwise you will distract your audience from the content of your presentation. They will all be thinking about the special effects instead.

On Target

In this unit you should have learnt how to:

■ plan and structure a presentation
■ use software to put together a series of slides to support a presentation
■ add multimedia features to the presentation
■ give a presentation.

WHAT YOU HAVE TO DO

■ **Give your presentation to your group.**
■ **Watch and listen to the presentations from the other pupils in your group.**

While you are watching the other presentations, think about these evaluation questions.

1. **What are the main points of the presentation?**
2. **What makes it interesting?**

5 In Control

A computer program is a series of stored commands. In this unit you will learn how to write simple computer programs.

On Target

You should already know:

■ the main commands needed to produce simple drawing effects using the **Logo** language

■ how to spot and correct errors

■ how to put commands in the right sequence to produce the effects you want.

In this unit you will revise these skills and learn about:

■ how to save time and effort with automatic repetition

■ creating your own customised commands

■ working with visual design

■ working with geometry and angles.

When you complete this unit you will create a simple computer game that you can play with friends.

Programming

All computer packages are created by programmers. They write the commands to make the computer work in a particular way. The commands are stored on a disk or a CD. You can buy the software and copy it onto your computer.

Then you can run the program and the computer will follow the stored instructions.

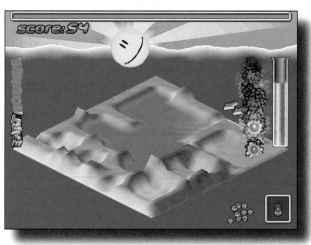

Computer games are an example of computer software.

The people who made the computer game planned every part of the game. Then they typed in all the commands that would make the game work:

● commands to control the screen display

● commands to do with how the player interacts with the game

● commands to do with scoring and winning the game.

Every single event on screen during the game has been planned and written by games programmers.

Automation

A computer program controls how a computer works. When a computer is controlled by a program it can carry on working even if nobody is there. Computer systems that work on their own are known as **automated** systems.

One of the simplest forms of automation is a *data logging* system. When a computer is used for data logging it measures and records environmental conditions using special measuring devices called *sensors*. It will carry on recording conditions even when there is nobody there to operate it.

- Find out whether your school computer system has any sensors available for you to use.
- If sensors are available, find out what you can measure with them.
- If possible use the sensors to log data for a 24-hour period. Keep the results in your IT folder.

A more complex program will run an automatic control system. A control system has two functions:

- it measures conditions
- it performs actions.

Here are some examples of control systems that have both these functions.

- A computer was programmed to detect movement in a room and turn on the burglar alarm.
- A computer was programmed to turn on the heating in a greenhouse when it got too cold.
- A computer was programmed to detect a car approaching and then raise a barrier.

If you want a computer to control events in the real world then the computer must be programmed to sense conditions and respond to them.

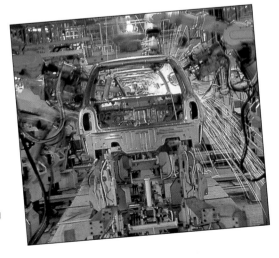

A robot must be able to react to the conditions around it in order to do its work. Real robots are found in factories, doing work like building cars

Logo

In this unit you will learn more about the programming language called **Logo**. Logo was invented more than thirty years ago. It was developed as a training language for young people to learn programming.

When you give commands in Logo the computer responds by moving a pointer on the screen. The pointer can draw shapes and write words on the screen. When you get good at Logo you can make the pointer draw multicoloured patterns, and you can make the computer work out the answer to questions and write the answers on the screen.

The first Logo programs were used to move a remote-controlled robot called a *Turtle*. People learning to program could type in commands, and see the turtle move.

The Logo you will learn in this unit moves a turtle on the screen, not a robot on the classroom floor.

Command Control

In Unit 1 of this book you learned that you interact with the computer by giving it instructions. In modern computer systems the main way to give instructions is through the graphical interface, by such actions as clicking and dragging. Throughout this book you have mainly used this type of control.

But in this unit you will learn how to control the computer by typing instructions. This gives you a greater range of commands, and it gives you tighter control over exactly what the computer does. The other advantage is that you can easily store the commands you give, in a computer file.

WHAT YOU HAVE TO DO

The companies who make computer games are always looking for new ideas.

Working alone or in a group, make notes about the possibilities for a new computer game. Where would it be set? Who would be the main character? What makes this game different from any others on sale?

I. At my command

On this page you will look at the programming language you will use for this unit, and some of the commands you can give.

A programming language

On this page you will learn how to give commands in the **Logo** programming language.

All the commands that control the movement of the turtle on the screen are shown on this page as well as the rules about how to use them.

Logo

Logo is a standard computer language. That means that although you can get different versions of Logo, made by different companies, they all work in much the same way.

The version of Logo used in this book as an example is called **Mach Turtles *Logo*.** Your teacher will tell you if you are using a different version, and what any differences are. You should be able to follow the work in this book easily, whatever version of Logo you use.

Mach Turtles Logo
Learning Edition

Version 1.00
This version expires June 30, 1999

Copyright © 1996-1998 Mach Turtles Software Inc. All rights reserved.

The Logo interface

The Logo interface will look something like this.

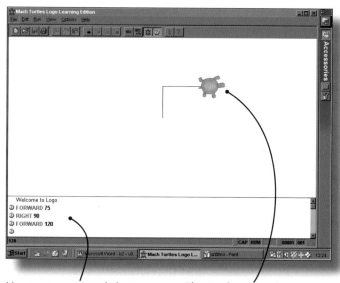

You type commands here   The turtle moves in response to your commands

As the turtle moves it leaves a line on the screen. It's as if it is holding a pen that writes on the ground as it walks.

Logo commands

Here are the basic Logo commands that you can use to move the turtle and draw on the screen.

CLEARSCREEN	**PENUP**
FORWARD *n*	**PENDOWN**
BACK *n*	
RIGHT *n*	
LEFT *n*	

In these commands *n* stands for any number.

Rules

There are very few rules about Logo. The computer will understand the commands as long as:

- you spell them properly
- you leave at least one space between the command and the number that follows it.

You can:

- use upper or lower case letters
- leave extra spaces in a command
- put more than one command on the same line.

Have you noticed that the command words are shown in blue? The Logo package does this automatically to show that it recognises these words.

Practise

To start giving **Logo** commands simply type a command in, and watch how the turtle moves. As you get good at it you can draw shapes like squares, rectangles and triangles on the screen.

Mistakes

If you make a mistake – for example spell a command wrongly – then you will see a simple error message.

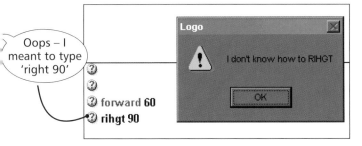

- Click on **OK** on the error message, and retype the command

Draw shapes

Here is a set of commands typed in by a pupil.

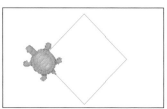

Just by reading these commands, can you tell what shape the turtle will draw on the screen?

- Type in these commands and see if your guess was right

Here is another shape drawn by the turtle.

What sequence of commands will produce this shape?

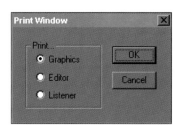

Print

To print out the results of any **Logo** work you do, pick **Print** from the **File** menu. You will see this window.

- Pick **Graphics** to print out the turtle track
- Pick **Listener** to print out the commands you gave

WHAT YOU HAVE TO DO

You should know how to control the turtle using Logo commands. Complete these tasks to practise your skills, and to demonstrate what you can do.

- **Enter the commands to make the computer draw a square on the screen.**
- **Enter the commands to make the computer draw a diamond shape on the screen.**

In both cases print out the turtle graphics and the sequence of commands. Keep your work in your IT folder.

2. Again and again

On this page you will learn how to cut out some of the time and effort by using the *Repeat* command.

Repeating yourself

Next you will learn about a new kind of Logo command. **Repeat** is a command that lets you draw large and complicated shapes with just one line of typing.

Hide the turtle

To see the shapes you draw more easily use this command:

HideTurtle

If you want to see the turtle again, type:

Showturtle

The short versions of these commands are:

Ht

St

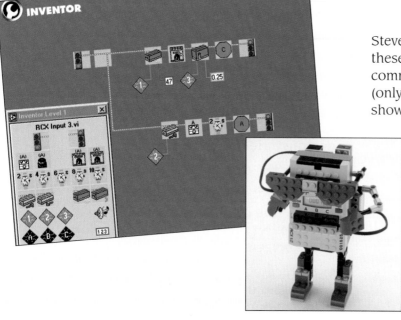

Forward n Right n ▪

Some pupils were experimenting to find out how many shapes they could draw using just two Logo commands: **Forward** and **Right**.

By carefully choosing the numbers they used with these commands they could draw all sorts of shapes.

Linda typed in these commands.

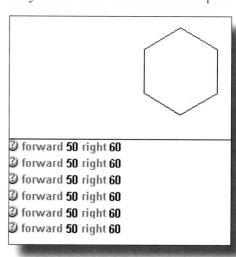

② forward **50** right **60**
② forward **50** right **60**
② forward **50** right **60**
② forward **50** right **60**
② forward **50** right **60**
② forward **50** right **60**

Steve typed in these commands (only a few are shown).

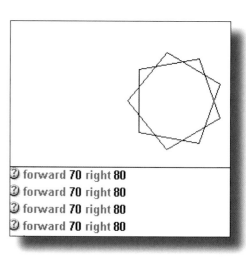

② forward **70** right **80**
② forward **70** right **80**
② forward **70** right **80**
② forward **70** right **80**

i Draw a star *p72*

Repeat

Instead of having to type the same command over and over again, you can use **repeat**.

The repeat command looks like this:

Repeat *x* [commands]

- Type the word **Repeat**
- Then type the number of repeats you want
- Then type the commands you want to repeat, inside square brackets

Steve was using this command:

forward 70 right 80

Instead of typing this command over and over again, he tried using the **repeat** command to save time.

This is Steve's work, showing the **Repeat** command

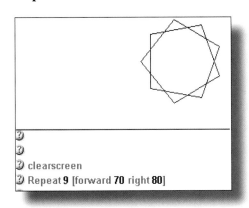

Leanne used a **Repeat** command to draw a square.

This is Leanne's work

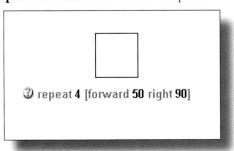

Now you try it. Use these commands:

Repeat

Forward

Right

You can draw a wide range of different shapes. Here are just some examples.

- See what shapes you can make

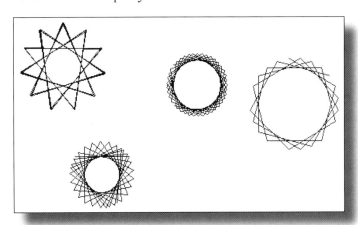

Game on

People who write computer programs use the **repeat** command a lot (or a command that works in much the same way). Next time you play a computer game look out for repeated actions. Typically a computer game will feature several key actions or events that happen over and over again.

Commands that are repeated are called **loops**, because the program loops back to where it was before.

```
Private Sub Command1_Click ()
    For Counter = 1 To 130
        Picture1.Move Picture1.Left + Counter
        Picture2.Move Picture2.Left + Counter
        PauseTime = 0.01
        Start = Timer
        Do While Timer < Start + PauseTime
            'do nothing
        Loop
    Next Counter
    For Counter = 1 To 130
        Picture1.Move Picture1.Left - Counter
    Next Counter
    End Sub
```

WHAT YOU HAVE TO DO

Create at least three different shapes with just one line of instructions each.

Print out the shapes you drew and the command line for each shape.

Remember to keep your work in your IT folder.

3. Getting into shape

On this page there are ideas for more work you can do with shapes.

Working with shapes

Here are some suggestions for further work:

- try different colours and line styles to change the appearance of shapes
- experiment with angles and maths to explore shapes.

You will look at some work completed by pupils, and compare what they did to the work of a programmer creating a new computer game.

To begin with you will look at some ideas for changing the colour and style of the shapes you draw.

Visuals in games programming ■

The programmers who make computer games have to use commands carefully to design the visual impact of the game.

Think of a computer game you have played. Did you think the appearance of the game was well designed?

Load a background picture ■

Mach turtles *Logo* includes some background scenes.

● Open the **File** menu and select **Import Picture**

Then pick the backgrounds you want.

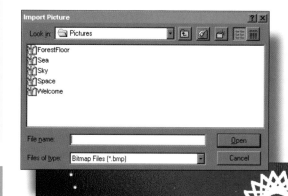

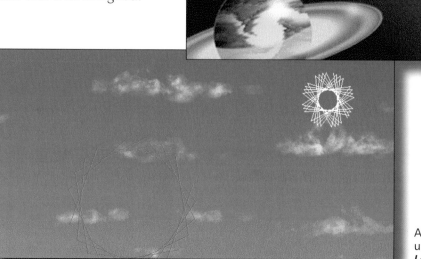

Artwork created using **Mach Turtles** *Logo*

Set Pen Colour

You can change the colour of the line the turtle draws with the command **SetPenColor**. Shorten this to

> **SetPC**

Here are some examples:

> **SetPC :red**
>
> **SetPC :blue**
>
> **Set PC :darkgray**

Set Pen Width

You can change the width of the line the turtle draws. The command is **SetPenWidth**, which can be shortened to

> **SetPW**

For example:

> **SetPW 1**
>
> **SetPW 5**

There are five widths. 1 is the narrowest, 5 is the widest.

Learning about angles

You can use Logo to explore and learn about angles.

Leanne tried out different angles. She typed the same command four times. All she changed was the final number.

> **Repeat 25 [Forward 100 Right 75]**
>
> **Repeat 25 [Forward 100 Right 88]**
>
> **Repeat 25 [Forward 100 Right 132]**
>
> **Repeat 25 [Forward 100 Right 150]**

By changing the angle of turn she created different shapes.

Investigate angles

Leanne found that, if the angle she chose for a shape divided exactly into 360, then the turtle returned to where it started after one circuit. The resulting shape is simple.

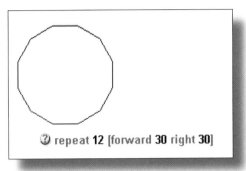

*repeat **12** [forward **30** right **30**]*

If she chose a number that would not divide exactly into 360 then the turtle took more than one circuit to return to where it started. The resulting shape is complex.

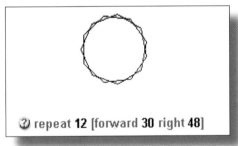

*repeat **12** [forward **30** right **48**]*

Angles in games programming

In games that involve actions like firing weapons, flying or driving vehicles, angles are very important. The programmers who make the games use angles to work out whether a shot hits its target, or whether a flying spaceship crashes.

Think of a computer game you have played. Note down one example where angles are used to work out a result.

WHAT YOU HAVE TO DO

Create a background scene for a space adventure game, with stars of different sizes and colours.

4. My word!

On this page you will learn how to teach the computer new commands of your own invention.

Teach the computer a new word

You have learned a wide range of Logo commands. You have practised using them to create different designs and visual effects.

An extra feature offered by Logo is that you are able to teach the computer new words. On this page you will learn how to do this.

You will also teach the computer how to place a *star* on the screen. On the next page you will use this new command to create a simple computer game that you and your friends can play.

The editor

So far you have used two parts of the Logo screen – the *graphics* area, where the turtle draws shapes, and the *listener* area, where you enter commands.

A third area is available, called the **editor**. You use the editor to define new commands.

In Mach Turtles *Logo* you use these buttons at the top of the screen to display the editor.

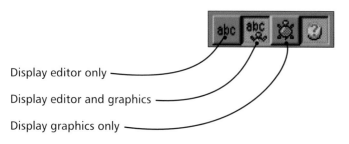

Display editor only

Display editor and graphics

Display graphics only

This screen shows all three Logo windows: the editor, the graphics area and the listener.

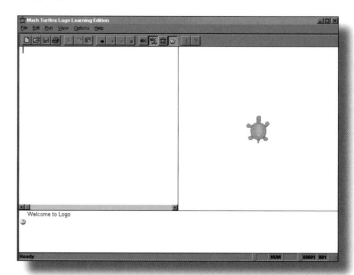

Draw a star

You are going to teach the computer how to draw a star.

First you must decide what kind of star you want. Here is an example.

You can use this example, or pick a star of your own design.

⑦ **repeat 12 [forward 40 left 150]**

Tell the computer how to star

Whatever star design you have chosen, type the command in the editor area like this.

- Type **To Star**
- Type the command(s) you want the computer to learn
- Type **End**

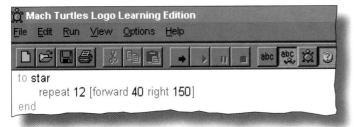

Load the definition

You have defined a word in the editor area. Now you have to load that definition so that you can use the word as a command.

- Open the **Run** menu
- Pick **Run From Start**

You should see this message in the *listener* area.

STAR defined.

Use the new word

The computer now knows what the word star means. Use this new word just like any other command.

- Enter this sequence of commands:

    ClearScreen

    PenUp

    Forward 250

    PenDown

    Star

More words

You can define more words in the editor window. Here a pupil has defined *star* and *square*.

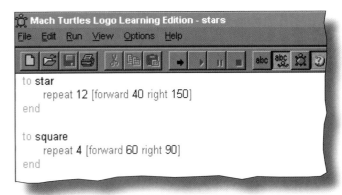

Print and Save

You can print out everything you have typed in the Editor.

- Pick **Print** from the **File** menu
- Pick **Editor** from the print window

You can also save all the definitions in the Editor

- Pick **Save** from the **File** menu
- Enter a suitable file name

Next time you use Logo, you can open the file where you stored the definitions:

- Pick **Open** from the **File** menu

Next load the definitions from the file:

- Pick **Run from Start** from the **Run** menu

Now you can use the words you defined in a previous lesson.

WHAT YOU HAVE TO DO

1. **Teach the computer the word** *star* **as shown on this page.**
2. **Use the new command to draw stars all over the screen.**
3. **Teach the computer the word** *square*.
4. **Print out the contents of the editor.**
5. **Save the words you have defined.**

Keep your work in your IT folder.

5. Star wars

Now you will learn how to use your Logo skills to create a simple computer game.

Create a simple computer game

Finally you need to create your computer game. The game works like this:

- the computer displays a star in a random position on the screen
- you *fire* the turtle at the star
- if the turtle ends up on top of the star then you win that round!

Pick a random point ■

On the last page you learned how to teach the computer a new command. You taught it the command *star*.

Use these same skills to teach the computer the command *randomplace*.

```
to randomplace

    hideturtle
    penup
    setx (random 600) - 300
    sety (random 300) - 150
    pendown

end
```

Remember to load the definitions from the editor, by opening the **Run** menu and picking **Run From Start**.

Draw a star in a random place ■

By combining the *randomplace* command and the *star* command you can make the computer draw a star at a random point on the screen.

Here is an example.

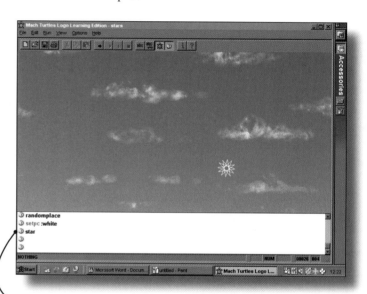

Enter the commands to draw a random star

Set the turtle ■

To complete the game you need one final command. The command is called 'set.turtle'. You are allowed to put a full stop in the middle of a command name if it makes the name clearer. This command positions the turtle at the bottom of the screen, in the middle, facing straight upwards.

```
to set.turtle

    showturtle
    penup
    setx 0
    sety - 180
    setheading 0

end
```

- Enter this command in the *Editor* window and teach it to the computer

i Teach the computer a new word *p72*

Start the game

Now you are ready to play the computer game.

- Load a background picture for the game (remember you can do this using the **File** menu, **Import picture** option).
- What colour and pen width will stand out well on this background picture? Use the **set pencolour** and **set penwidth** commands to pick a suitable line style.

Now you are ready to play the game. Enter these commands.

> **Randomplace**
>
> **Star**
>
> **Set.turtle**

These commands will:

- pick a random place on the screen
- draw a star in that place
- move the turtle to the bottom of the screen.

Get your friend to type in two commands and see where the turtle ends up. Did the turtle touch the star?

Now you can play a second time.

- Enter the three commands that set up the game: **randomplace**, **star** and **set.turtle**
- Using only **right** or **left** and **forward** try to shoot the turtle so that it touches the star.

You can play as many rounds as you like.

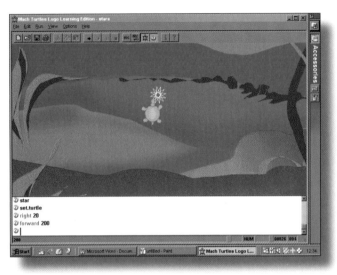

One round of the game

Save time

To make it even easier you can teach the computer one final command called *Play*.

Now every time you type *Play* the computer will get ready for the next round of the game.

```
to play

    randomplace
    star
    set.turtle

end
```

Play the game

Challenge a friend to play this game. Here are the rules.

1. You can enter only two Logo commands.
2. You can enter one **right** or **left** command to turn the turtle.
3. You can enter one **forward** command to make the turtle walk.
4. If the turtle ends up touching the star then you get a point.

WHAT YOU HAVE TO DO

1. **Create the game shown on this page by following the instructions.**
2. **Play the game with a friend.**
3. **Print out the commands you have used.**

Keep your work in your IT folder.

6. Data collection

On the last page of this unit you will look at how computer systems are used to sense and control events.

Control and data logging

You have used a sequence of commands to control the **Logo** turtle. You have seen how real programmers use similar techniques. The example used in this unit was games programming.

On this page you will look at a different type of control system – one which senses conditions in the real world, and responds to them.

Sensors

Nowadays it is possible to build equipment to measure conditions in the environment. Here are some examples.

- Measure the temperature in a room
- Measure the wind speed on a hillside
- Measure the amount of electric current in a wire
- Measure the acidity of a solution

Sensors like this measure conditions and convert the measurements to an electronic signal. The electronic signal can then be fed into a computer.

Data logging

The computer can keep a record of the signals from the sensors. The signals are electronic numbers, representing conditions. These numbers can be stored like any other set of numbers inside the computer.

When the computer works automatically to record the information from sensors, this is called **data logging**. One of the most important things about data logging is that it works automatically. There doesn't have to be anyone there.

You could read a thermometer every hour and type the result into a computer. This wouldn't be data logging.

Or you could use a sensor that read the temperature, and fed the result into the computer. This would be data logging because it could go on day and night, working on its own.

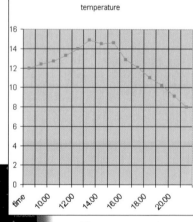

The computer has logged and recorded the air temperature throughout a typical spring day

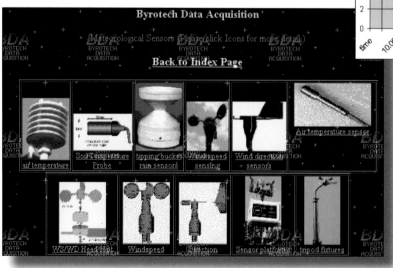

These sensors are used by meteorologists to detect weather conditions

Advantages of data logging ■

Why use data logging? Here are some advantages:

- you don't have to be there, so you can get on with other things
- you can keep a record on conditions for hours or days, and the computer never gets bored
- the computer never misreads the signals from the sensors
- sensors can detect conditions where no human can go – for example inside a volcano or on the surface of the moon.

Where no one has gone before

The Mars Polar Lander is an example of data logging. It is equipped with a wide range of sensors, which it uses to detect conditions on the surface of Mars.

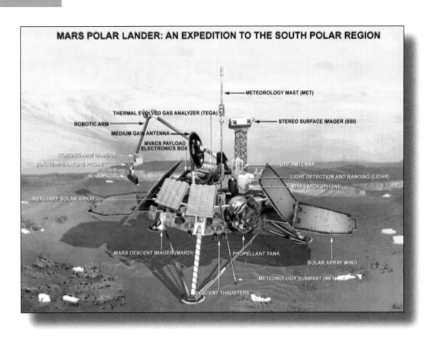

An artist's impression of the Mars Polar Lander

"Autotest" Control and Data Logging Computer

Cussons Autotest has been purpose designed to meet the complex and demanding control and data management requirements of current engine test facilities engaged in both routine testing operations and advanced research work. The system is provided as a compact package using a conventional 19 inch mounting system for convenient installation within existing or new facilities. Utilising the latest Motorola 68030 series processor family and the state of the art high level "C" programming language for the source code, a particularly powerful yet flexible system has resulted.

Control ■

You have seen how computers can be used to detect and record conditions. Some computer systems go one step further. They use the data they collect from sensors to control equipment.

A very simple example would be a heating control. The computer could detect the temperature of a room, and turn the central heating on or off, depending on how hot it was in the room.

You will be doing more about data logging and control later in your IT course.

On Target

You have completed the unit on programming and control. You should know how to:

- use commands to control the movement of the turtle as it draws on the screen
- use repeat to save time and effort
- teach the computer new commands
- work with visual design and angles
- put commands together to create a working program.

WHAT YOU HAVE TO DO

1. **Name three different measurements that can be made by the sensors shown on this page**

2. **What are the disadvantages of using data logging to record conditions on Mars? What advantages are there to sending a manned mission?**

3. **What programming language is used in the control system illustrated on this page?**

UNIT

INTRODUCTION

6 Searching for Information

In this unit you will learn how to find a wealth of useful information by searching a CD-ROM.

On Target

You should already know:

- how to navigate between the screens of displayed information
- how to make simple use of information taken from a CD-ROM
- about copyright.

In this unit you will revise these skills and learn about:

- how a CD-ROM stores information
- how to recognise and use the key features of a CD-ROM interface to find what you want
- finding and using multimedia
- making the most of interactive features.

You can use the items that you find on a CD-ROM to help with work in graphics, document production, and giving presentations.

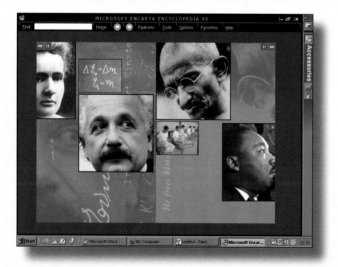

What's on a CD-ROM?

The feature that makes a CD-ROM so useful is that it can store a great deal of information. It can store any type of information that the computer can hold.

- Words and numbers
- Graphics and photographs
- Sounds
- Video and animation

On a typical CD you will find all of these types of information.

Sound, pictures and text combine to present information on **World Languages** (above) and **Influential people of the 20th Century** (left)

Getting IT Right in...

Art

Pupils in an Art class were learning about famous paintings. A CD-ROM from the Louvre art gallery in Paris let them look at examples of famous paintings. The navigation tools meant that it was quick and easy to find different paintings by different artists and from different periods.

The CD-ROM also offered them information about the paintings. You can see some examples in this picture, for example a **time-line** is available to show how this painting fits into the history of painting.

These pupils didn't have the opportunity to visit Paris for themselves, but at least the CD-ROM gave them a chance to see some of the most famous paintings in the world.

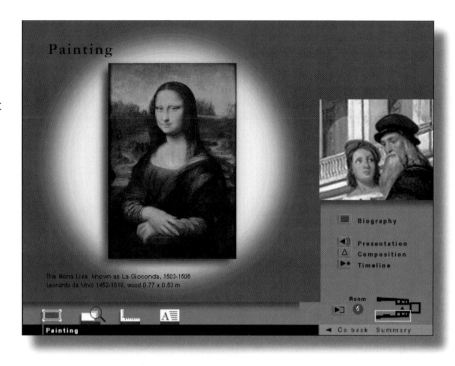

The *Mona Lisa* on a CD-ROM (© *Montparnasse Multimedia* 1995)

Interactivity

When you use a CD-ROM you don't simply read what it contains, as you would read a book. Instead you take an active role. For example, you can:

- search for information
- take part in activities
- test yourself with a quiz
- play learning games
- explore alternatives.

Making use of IT

When you have found information on a CD-ROM you can use it in a number of ways. Because the information is in computerised form you can make use of it in your own computer work. For example, you can:

- read and make notes
- copy pictures into documents
- incorporate sound and video into presentations
- extract numbers for use in calculations.

The example of a CD-ROM used in this unit is **Microsoft Encarta**.
This is a multimedia encyclopedia.

Encarta Encyclope...

Encarta contains a wide range of information. It includes many activities. The interface shows many of the features that help you to work with CD-ROMs.

There are many different versions of *Encarta*. The example used in this book is *Encarta 99*. If you use a different version it may look slightly different. There are plenty of other encyclopedias, and there are other types of CD-ROM which contain useful information. If you use one of these alternatives, it will obviously have a different interface.

It doesn't matter what CD-ROM you choose to use for this unit. What you should be looking out for is general features and methods.

IT at work

As well as visual and text information a CD-ROM can hold sound samples.

This CD-ROM allows you to take sound samples and combine them to create new compositions.

Modern electronic music is often put together without the use of instruments. The musicians take samples of music, for example from CD-ROMs, and mix them using computer software.

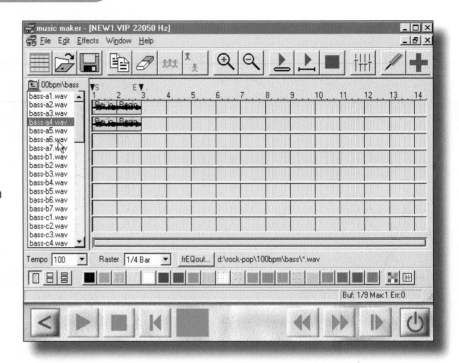

i Searching for information p84

How IT helps

Taking information from a CD-ROM can help to improve your schoolwork.

- Exploring ideas on a CD-ROM can help you to think about what you are learning and the work you have to do.
- Extracting materials from a CD-ROM can make your work more exciting and attractive.
- A CD-ROM can provide information that you can't get from anywhere else.

People and the weather

In this unit you will see how pupils in a Geography class used a CD-ROM to help them with their study of *People and the Weather*. They watched a TV series on the subject and did some preparatory work. Then they were split into groups. Each group had to pick a topic for research, related to *People and the Weather*.

Leah and Tom decided to look at *hurricanes*, *tornadoes* and other types of *storm*. They were interested in how these storms were formed, and they also wanted to look at the effect of severe storms on people who live in areas subject to such weather conditions.

Jack, Suzie and Robyn wanted to study the way *climate* varies in different countries and cities, and how it affects the lives of people living in different parts of the world.

Rose, Rita and Raksha were interested in art and colour. They decided to pick a topic that would let them look at colour, and create attractive images. They picked *rainbows* as a topic. Their teacher told them they would have to find out about the science of rainbows as well as just drawing pretty pictures.

David, Iain, Carl and Alice decided to look at how people live in conditions of extreme *cold*. They had two lines of enquiry: they wanted to look at the modern Inuit people of the extreme North. They also wanted to look at the Ice Age, and how people lived in those days.

Tracey and Monica said they wanted to study the effect that people have on the weather. They picked the *greenhouse effect* as a topic.

WHAT YOU HAVE TO DO

1. Go to your school library or resource centre and find out what CD-ROMs are available. Ask if they have a list of available CD-ROMs.

2. Find out what the arrangements are for pupils who want to use CD-ROMs. Are any available on the school network?

3. Find out if your local library has any CD-ROMs.

Write notes about what you find and keep them in your IT folder.

I. About interface

On this page you will look at an example of a CD-ROM and the software interface that enables you to use it.

The CD-ROM interface

The **interface** of a computer system or a software package means the facility that allows you to use it. The interface:

- lets you perform actions and control the system
- lets the computer communicate information to you.

Here you will see how some pupils used this encyclopedia to help with work they were doing in Geography about people and the weather.

Screens

A book is organised into pages. A CD-ROM is organised into **screens**. To move from screen to screen you click on links.

The main or start-up screen of a CD-ROM is usually called the **Home** screen. From the Home screen you can explore any part of the CD-ROM. Below is the Home screen of *Encarta*.

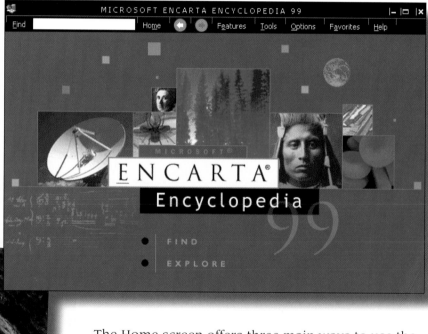

The Home screen offers three main ways to use the CD-ROM:

- Find
- Explore
- Features

You can use similar facilities with almost any CD-ROM. When you start up a CD-ROM, have a look at the Home screen first and see what it contains.

If you have a copy of *Encarta*, you can follow the task through with the pupils. Or you could choose another encyclopedia-type CD-ROM.

Find

The **Find** facility lets you search for particular words. There are two aspects to the **Find** facility:

- word search
- index.

- Look for word searches and indexes on the CD-ROM that you are using

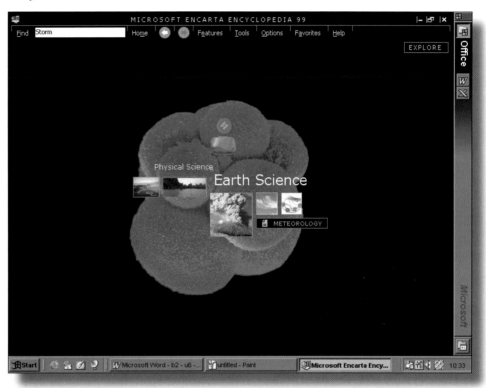

The **Explore** feature lets you look at information by subject. This screen lets you explore Earth Science which covers Geology, earthquakes and the weather

Explore

The **Explore** facility is equivalent to the *Contents* page of a book. It presents the content of the CD-ROM organised by topics.

- Look for **Contents** or a list of main topics on the CD-ROM you are using

Features

Features are special interactive ways of making use of the CD-ROM. Examples of features include:

- time-lines
- maps
- activities
- games.

Look for special features and activities on the CD-ROM you are using. Learn more about special features on the next page.

WHAT YOU HAVE TO DO

Start up the CD-ROM that you are studying.

1. Note down its name and the type of information it contains. Is it a general encyclopedia? Or is it concerned with a particular topic?

2. Look at the Home screen. Try to identify the functions that help you to use the CD-ROM.

3. Which of these does it have?

   ■ Index

   ■ Word search

   ■ Topic-based organisation (for example a Contents screen)

   ■ Special features

   ■ Activities

Put your notes about the CD-ROM and its Home screen into your IT folder.

2. Search for the hero

Next you will see how pupils found information about people and the weather on the CD-ROM.

Searching for information

If you want to use the information on a CD-ROM to help with your work then the first thing is to find it. There is a lot of information on a typical CD-ROM. It is important to *zoom in* on the information you want.

CD-ROMs offer several ways for you to search.

- Index
- Word search (often combined with the index)
- Contents or Topics
- Special features

Index ■

One of the options on the *Encarta* Home screen is **Find**.

- Click on **Find** to see the Index

An index lists all the articles in the dictionary, in alphabetical order.

- Scroll down the index to the words beginning with a 'W'. You can see the articles about the weather in this list

- Click on one of the index entries to see an article on the weather

Word search ■

At the top of the index is a **word search**. If you type in a word here then the computer will search for:

- articles with that word in the title
- articles with that word anywhere in the article.

Leah and Tom were investigating storms, including hurricanes and tornadoes. They used the word search facility. The first word they entered was *Tornado*.

This symbol means there is a picture available

There were three articles on tornadoes, and lots that contained the word *tornado*. They followed the links to pictures and found these two.

American Red Cross

Howard Bluestein/Science Source/Photo Researchers, Inc.

- Your CD-ROM will probably have an index and a word search. Find out how to see them, and how to use them

Contents

Jack, Suzie and Robyn wanted to study the way climate varies in different countries. A useful resource would be a world map with the different types of climate shown.

They decided to use the **Explore** option. This organises the work by topic, like the *Contents* page of a book.

- Click on the **Explore** option
- Follow the topic links to Science and Physics
- Find the section on Earth Science (Geology and Meteorology)

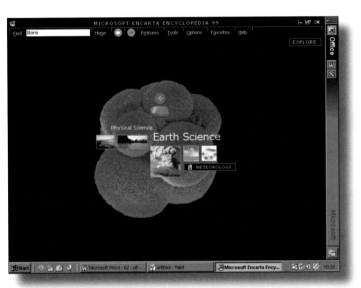

They found this map.

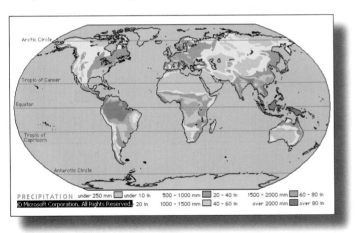

Your CD-ROM probably has a *Contents* or a topic listing. Find out how to see this topic listing, and how to use it to look through the CD-ROM.

Other encyclopedias

There are lots of different encyclopedias available on CD-ROM. Some are designed for young people, or for general family use. Others are more detailed, and designed mainly for adults.

All CD-ROM encyclopedias offer you an interface with a range of useful features

WHAT YOU HAVE TO DO

You must choose a topic for your investigation of a CD-ROM. The topic you choose depends on the subjects covered by your CD-ROM.

1. **Pick a topic, and check with your teacher that you can use it.**

2. **Explore the search facilities on your CD-ROM and see what you can find out about your chosen topic.**

3. **If you have time, go straight on to the next page to find out what you can do with the information once you find it.**

3. Copy right

On the previous page you saw how pupils found the information they wanted. Here you will see how to make use of the information that you find.

Making use of what you find

What can you do with the information on a CD-ROM? That's the subject of this page. You will see how pupils made use of what they found. They did this in three main ways:

- reading and making notes
- copying
- printing.

Try to do similar actions to those shown here, using your own CD-ROM and investigating the topic you chose on the last page.

Reading and making notes

On the previous page you saw that Leah and Tom were investigating storms using the word search option. They found the article shown below.

This screen contains a lot of interesting information. They read it through, using the scroll bar, and made notes. They noted the main facts from the article, to help them remember them.

● Make notes from an article you have found

Once you have made notes you can use them to write an essay, for example.

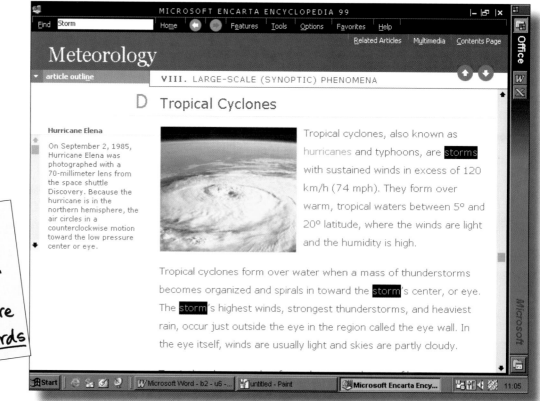

Handwritten notes:

Hurricanes
Winds over 70mph
Northern hemisphere, anti-clockwise
Centre - low pressure
Winds spiral inwards

Copy

Rose, Rita and Raksha were finding out about rainbows. Using the **Explore** function they found this article.

- Open the **Options** menu to copy or print what you see

The pupils picked **Copy** from this menu. Then they *pasted* the picture into their Geography report.

- Copy or print out one of the images you have found in your search

Copyright

Copyright is the law that means you can't take a copy of anybody else's work without permission. It applies to making computer copies of items from CD-ROMs. On the right is what the *Encarta Encyclopedia* has to say about copyright.

Microsoft also says this about *Encarta* materials:

'You may copy text and images from *Encarta Encyclopedia* for your personal use only. Copyright law does not allow you to copy an article, or image for commercial publication, or for posting onto a computer bulletin board or web site.'

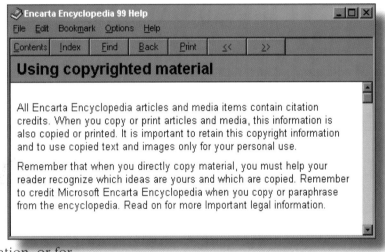

Do you understand what this means for your work?

- You can copy things from the CD-ROM into your own work.
- You must make sure you say where you got the information, and distinguish it from your own work.
- You can't use it to make anything for commercial use or on an Internet web site.

- Find out what it says about copyright on the CD-ROM you are using

WHAT YOU HAVE TO DO

On the last page you found information on a particular topic.

1. **Make notes from some of the text you have found.**

2. **Print out one of the images you have found.**

3. **Find out what the rules on copyright are, and write them down in your own words.**

Put your notes, the picture and your explanation of copyright into your IT folder.

4. Thunder and lightning

You looked at multimedia in the unit on presentations. This page is about the multimedia samples you can find on CD-ROMs.

Finding and using multimedia

CD-ROMs are usually a rich source of multimedia materials. On this page you will look at the multimedia samples available on a CD-ROM – how to find them and how to use them.

Once you find multimedia samples you can use them in two main ways:

- run the sound or video and learn from it
- copy the sound or video into a presentation.

The pupils used multimedia found on *Encarta* in both these ways. On this page you can see what they did. Try to follow this work for yourself with your CD-ROM.

Searching for multimedia

You can look for whatever type of multimedia you want by using the **search** feature.

With this feature you can list all the multimedia clips, or find clips on a particular topic.

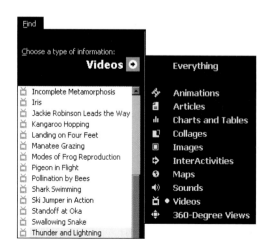

Sounds

Listening to sound clips can teach you new things. For example you can hear the sounds that different animals make.

David, Iain, Carl and Alice were studying people who live in very cold climates. They were interested in the life of the Inuit people. They found useful sound clips on the CD-ROM. They found samples of Inuit songs and learned some Inuit words.

Sounds can also be used to enhance your presentations if you can copy them. *Encarta* does not let you make copies of sounds onto your own computer system.

- Play some sounds on your chosen topic
- Note down what sounds you have listened to

Animation

An example of an **animation** is a cartoon. A series of images are presented in sequence very quickly. This makes it look like they move. Some CD-ROMs include animations to help you learn difficult concepts.

Tracey and Monica were investigating the greenhouse effect. They found an animation that explained the greenhouse effect using moving diagrams.

This animation helped them to understand the greenhouse effect more easily.

- Look for animations on your CD-ROM
- Watch an animation and make notes on what you have learned from it

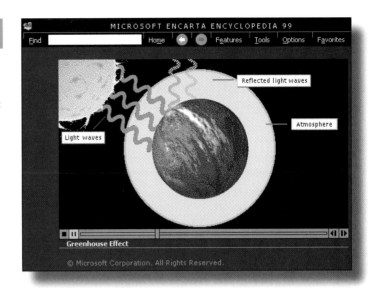

This animation shows the light waves travelling from the Sun to the Earth, and being trapped by the atmosphere. This is a still picture from the animation

Video

Video clips are short pieces of live action films. It can be more useful to see a moving image than a still photograph.

Leah and Tom were still looking for information about people and storms. They found this video clip showing a thunderstorm in Africa.

The film used fast-forward photography to show how storm clouds built up. By watching this film the pupils learned more than they would have from looking at still photographs.

- Find video clips on your CD-ROM
- Watch at least one film clip and make notes of what you saw

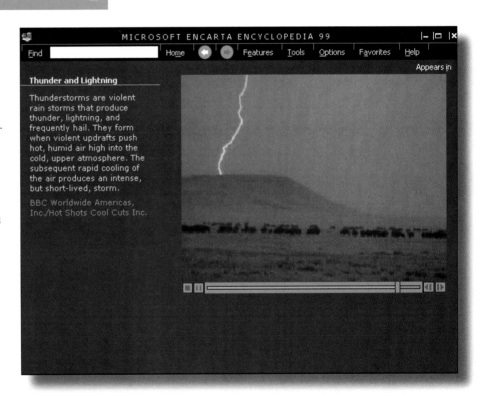

Sometimes you can copy animations and videos into your presentations, but this facility is not offered with *Encarta*.

What do you think?
Multimedia clips are fun, but how useful are they? You have looked at (and listened to) some multimedia clips.

- Do you think you have learned anything from them?
- Do you think they are worth bothering with?
- Which clips did you find most useful?

WHAT YOU HAVE TO DO

1. **Look for multimedia clips on your chosen topic, and watch or listen to them.**

2. **Note down what clips you have found.**

3. **Explain how these clips helped you to learn about your chosen topic.**

5. Just in time

On the final page in this unit you will see how you can carry out interactive activities provided with a CD-ROM.

Activities and interaction

Another interesting feature offered on many CD-ROMs is the chance to do something active.

For example:

- do a test to see how much you know
- complete an active learning task
- find information using maps or time-lines
- check the effect of making changes.

If possible, follow the interactive activities on your CD-ROM.

Features

The **Features** menu of *Encarta* offers some interesting ways of finding information.

- Find out what special features there are on your CD-ROM

Time-lines

A time-line shows events and other information, organised in date order.

David, Iain, Carl and Alice were investigating how people live in very cold conditions. During the Ice Age it was very cold in Europe, and cave men survived in the extreme cold. They found a time-line feature on the CD-ROM and used it to look back in time to the Ice Age.

The time-line told them that the first animals were domesticated, and the first cities built, just after the end of the Ice Age. They clicked on the pictures to find out more about these events.

- Find out if there is a time-line available on your CD-ROM

If there is a time-line, is it helpful to the topic you are studying?

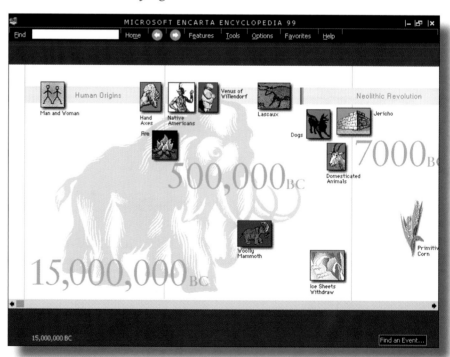

Activities

Encarta offers several **activities**.

Jack, Suzie and Robyn were studying the way climate varies. They found an activity relating to variations in climate between different cities. This feature let them pick cities and compare their temperature and rainfall.

They found this feature was most useful if they asked their teacher to help them. She told them about how cities close to the sea had different weather conditions from cities that were far inland. They spent time with a map, finding out where the cities were, and then looking at their weather.

You might find that activities are more rewarding if you discuss them with other people, or tie them in with other things you have learned.

- Find out if there are any activities on your chosen topic
- Complete an activity, and make notes on what you did

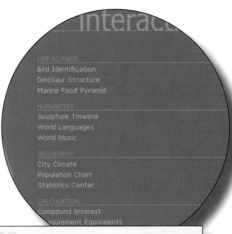

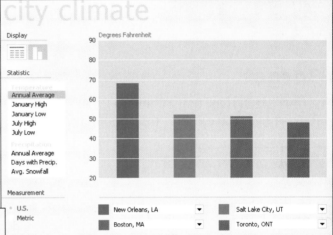

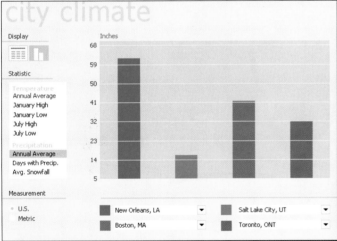

On Target

You have now completed the unit on searching through a CD-ROM. You should know how to:

- find the information you need
- use the information to enhance your work
- use interactive features to develop ideas.

WHAT YOU HAVE TO DO

Find out if there are any activities on the CD-ROM that will help you to investigate your chosen topic.

Do the activity, whatever it is.

Try to put the activity into context, rather than just doing it without discussing it with anyone. Work on the activity with other pupils and discuss what you do with your teacher.

Write something about the activity and what you learned from it. Do you think it was enjoyable? Do you think it was useful?

Put what you have written into your IT folder.

7 On the Internet

In this unit you will learn how to use the Internet to find useful and interesting materials to help you with your work.

On Target

The **Internet** is a system that connects computers all over the world. You should already know:

- how to use Internet browser software
- how to use a Search Engine to find web sites
- how to download information to your own computer.

In this unit you will revise these skills and learn how to:

- use the Internet to enhance your work
- explore web sites with a critical eye
- obtain information in a variety of forms
- search effectively for the items you need.

You will look at some examples of work from pupils investigating a local ecology system. You will see how their practical activities and their use of the Internet were combined to produce a richer overall experience. You can follow this work for yourself, using your own Internet research.

What is the Internet?

The Internet works by using communication links to share information between computers. Nobody is in charge of the Internet. Anybody who wants to can put information on the Internet.

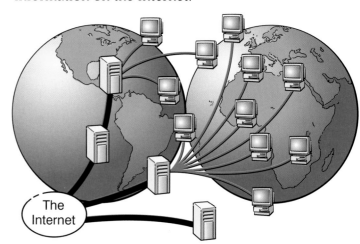

The Internet

The World Wide Web

The most useful feature of the Internet, and the one you will learn about in this unit, is called the **World Wide Web**. This is the collection of all the web sites in the world.

A web site is a collection of information that you can display on your computer screen. People all over world make web sites and connect them to the Internet. If you have Internet connection you can look at these web sites.

Why do people make web sites? Some do it for fun, as a hobby. Some do it for commercial reasons, for instance to sell or advertise products. Some do it to provide a public service.

 i What's on a CD-ROM? *p78*   Connecting to a site *p96*   Sources of information *p93*

IT at work

Internet web sites are created by web programmers. Some people make a web site for a hobby in their spare time. But, for other people, creating web sites is a full-time job.

Many large organisations think it is important to maintain a high-quality web site. The content of the web site is updated regularly. The web site is like a magazine that changes every week or month. This means that there is plenty of work for the *site manager* to do.

He or she is constantly looking out for new items to put on the web site. The site manager will also add new interactive features, such as a *site index* to help you to find what you want on the site.

beeb.com is an on-line magazine for young people from the BBC. Here is one part of the site, the section on *Top of the Pops*.

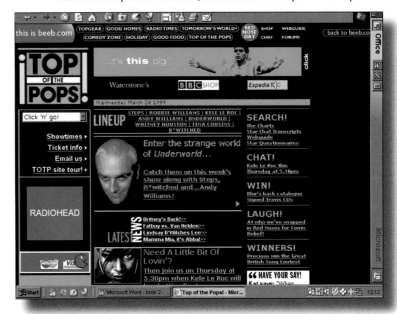

Sources of information

The main function of the Internet is as a source of **information**. Remember information can mean words, pictures and multimedia items.

Where else can you find information? The three main sources you might have used up to now are:

- books
- magazines and newspapers
- CD-ROMs.

How does the Internet compare with these other sources of information? It has **advantages** and **disadvantages**.

See more about these on the next page.

KidNews is a web site of news reports and other writing by young people. The URL for this site is: www.kidnews.com

The Internet offers three main advantages:

- wide range
- being up to date
- ease of access.

Compared to books or magazines the Internet offers a wider range of materials. On the Internet you can find multimedia items which are not available from a book.

The second advantage is that the Internet is changing everyday. This means that you can find very up-to-date information on the Internet. A CD-ROM offers multimedia materials, but obviously it does not change and so it may become out of date.

A multimedia web site. Its URL is: www.mamamedia.com

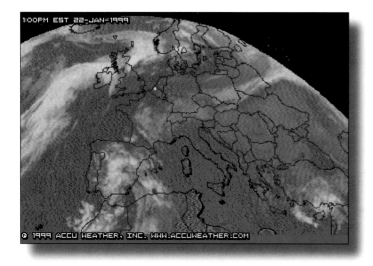

A satellite image of today's weather is just one example of up-to-date information

The third advantage is ease of access. Of course it is easy for you to access the books that are available in your home or classroom. But if you need books on a new subject it can be difficult, and expensive, to get hold of them.

Getting IT Right in...

Food Technology

Finding information on the Internet can support practical work you do in any subject.

For example pupils in a Food Technology class used the Internet to search for information about food and recipes from all over the world.

Disadvantages of the Internet

Of course the Internet has disadvantages too.

The first disadvantage is that it is so big. There are millions of items on the Internet. The problem can be finding items that are useful to you.

The second disadvantage is that the Internet is very variable. There is excellent and reliable material on the Internet, but there is also misleading and incorrect information.

In this unit you will see how to overcome these disadvantages. You will learn how to find worthwhile information that is suitable for your needs.

You will learn to use web sites that help you to find the information you want

Reliable or not?

Remember, anybody can make a web site. Some sites are excellent sources of worthwhile information. But some sites have information that is wrong. Other sites are controversial, that is people disagree about the information they provide.

For this reason you have to be careful. You have to think for yourself. Use your common sense, and think about what you find on the Internet.

True or not? The existence of *Bigfoot* in the USA is still a matter of debate

WHAT YOU HAVE TO DO

Three pupils have three different problems: but how can the Internet help them?

1. **Angela is writing a report about South America. She wants a picture of a modern city in South America, but all her books are at least ten years old.**

2. **Nathan is making a presentation about greyhound racing. His teacher has suggested that he liven it up with some sound or moving images. But where can he find computer files of a suitable kind?**

3. **Sharon is writing a report on nuclear power. She wants to know all the arguments, for and against, but how can she find lots of different opinions?**

Write notes explaining how the Internet could be a useful resource for each of these pupils. Explain what advantages the Internet offers over other sources of information.

Keep your work in your IT folder.

I. I should be so yucky

On this page you will see how to look at the web sites that are available over the Internet.

Connecting to a site

Web browser software

A software package that lets you connect to a web site over the Internet is called a **web browser**. The web browser used as an example in this unit is called **Microsoft *Internet Explorer*.** There are other packages, and they all work in the same way. You should be able to follow this unit, whatever package you use.

Internet Explorer

Using a web browser

When you start up a web browser package it looks like this.

Enter an address here   The web site will be displayed here

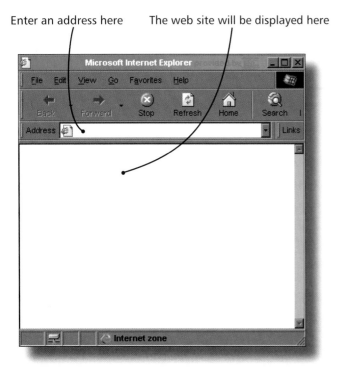

Address

At the top of the web browser there is room to enter a web site address.

Every web site has a unique address called a **URL** (pronounce it by saying the three letters *You – Ar – El*).

When you type a URL into the web browser the computer will:

- connect to the web site
- download the web site onto your computer.

Connect and download

The web site is held on a computer somewhere in the world. When you enter the URL you connect to that distant computer through an Internet connection.

The contents of the web site are **downloaded**. That means they are copied down the Internet connection onto your computer. When they have been copied onto your computer you can look at them in the working area of your web browser.

Web sites are nothing new - I've had mine for years.

i   On the Internet *p92*

Get yucky!

Some pupils were investigating ecological systems. They investigated an ecology that was very close at hand – the community of small creatures, like insects and worms, inhabiting the school playing fields. They went out and did practical work, finding creatures and examining them and their habitats.

They also looked on the Internet for information about the creatures they found. Their teacher gave them a starting point. They were given the URL for a site called *Yucky*. This is a site for young people, presenting facts about Science with emphasis on everything disgusting, slimy and, in short, yucky.

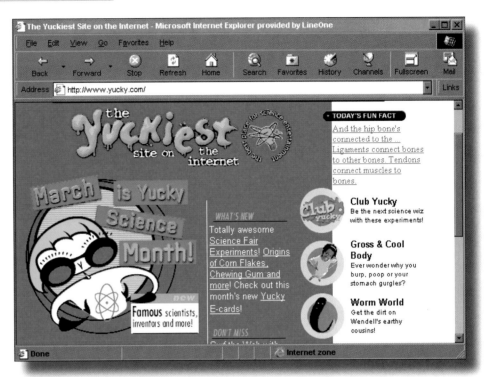

The URL for *Yucky* is

www.yucky.com

The pupils started up the web browser software. They typed this URL and downloaded the web site.

Not a book

An Internet web site is completely different to a book. A book stays the same, but a web site changes all the time. The contents of the web site this month may not be the same as the contents last month.

In fact, the best web sites are often those that change the quickest. That's because people are employed full-time to work on the sites, putting on new information every hour, day or month.

If you connect to *Yucky* you will probably find it looks different from the picture here. That's because it is an exciting, live site.

WHAT YOU HAVE TO DO

Away from the computer

Look out for URLs on TV, in magazines, and in other places. As a class make a list of web site addresses. This can be a class *web site directory*.

On the computer

Connect to the *Yucky* Science site, and see how it compares in appearance to the picture on this page.

Connect to any other sites in the class directory.

If you have time, go on to the next page in this book for more work to do on web sites.

2. Yucky sites

It's easy to move around the Internet using links. Can you learn how?

Click and link

On this page you will see how to use the Internet. You will see how to move about between different web sites, and what to do with the information you find.

Explore a web site

A web site is usually made of much more than one screen full of words and pictures. So to take a proper look at it you need to move around the site, looking at all the different screens.

You move around a web site, like *Yucky*, by clicking on **links**. A link can be a word, a picture, an arrowhead, or anything else. It is usually highlighted or labelled as a link.

These are links

Follow the links

You can follow links at random, picking those that look most interesting, or you can have a particular topic clearly in mind, and stick to that.

Both these approaches have got advantages:

- a **focused** search for a particular topic gets you where you want to go more quickly, with fewer distractions
- a more open **exploration** might take longer, but you might stumble on something completely unexpected and exciting.

Some pupils dug up some worms during their ecology investigation. The next day they went to *Yucky* and followed links to find out more about worms.

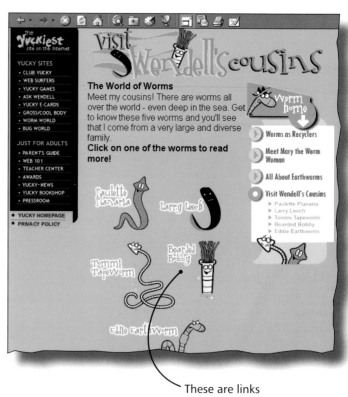

These are links

Every picture of a worm on this page is a link to a new screen with information on that worm.

The pupils had dug up earthworms. Perhaps they should have followed links to the *Earthworm* section. But they couldn't resist reading the section on *Tapeworms*. They thought this was probably the most revolting section of the whole site.

On the next page you will see what you can do when you find useful information on the Internet. You will see what the pupils did with another disgusting collection of information and pictures.

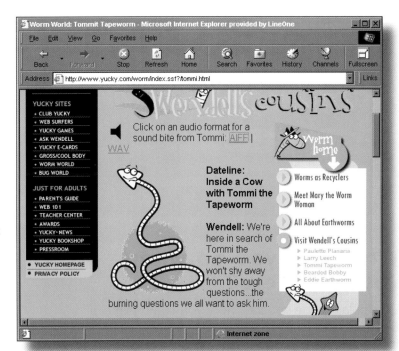

Moving between sites

The *Yucky* site also includes links to other sites elsewhere on the Internet. This screen shows links to other sites, recommended by young people.

Can you see the links on this page? They are the blue URLs. If you clicked on one of these you would move directly to the site.

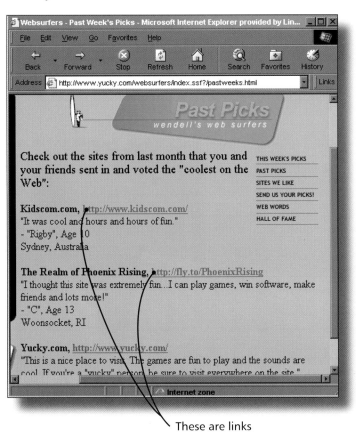

These are links

The Kidscom site – why not check it out?

WHAT YOU HAVE TO DO

Pick a Science topic. If you haven't got any other topics to investigate, pick worms, insects, or other small creatures.

- Follow links within the *Yucky* site.

- Enter any of the URLs you have collected in the class directory (see last page).

Use the **focused** approach or the **exploration** approach, and see what you find. If you have time, go on to the next page for ideas of things to do with the sites you find.

3. Larry Leech's page

So, you have followed links and found a site or a screen that you like. What can you do next?

What can you do when you get there?

On the last page you saw how you could explore a web site, or look at different web sites, by following **links**.

On this page you will look at what you can do with the web sites that you find.

You will see how pupils studying ecology used web site materials to help them with a presentation. Try to follow their actions yourself. But remember two things:

- the *Yucky* site changes all the time, so you won't find exactly the same information that is shown on this page. If you wish, pick a different site, or investigate a different topic from the one shown on this page

- you don't have to use the information you find to make a presentation, of course. You can use information on web sites to help with any kind of school work – for example an illustrated report with lots of interesting facts and colourful pictures.

Be critical

The first rule to remember is *be critical*. Don't take what you find on the Internet at face value. Ask yourself these questions.

- Who made this web site?
- Might they have a bias I should bear in mind?
- Could they be mistaken?
- Could be they be misleading?

The *Yucky* site is an educational site. But other sites are set up to sell products, to support particular points of view, or just as jokes.

Take notes

If you are reasonably happy with the content of a site then a good starting point is to take notes of what you find there. Some sites have a lot of text in them. Read such a site like a book, and note down the most interesting facts you find.

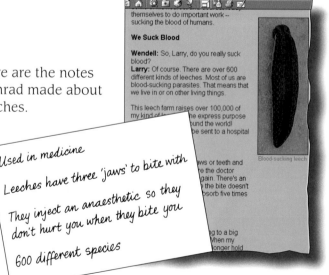

Leeches

Some pupils used hand held-nets to dip in the school pond. One of them found a leech. He put it in a jar for an hour and studied it with magnifying lenses.

This was an excellent topic for an ecology presentation. The group decided to find out about leeches. The teacher recommended that they use the Internet as a source of material for the presentation.

Here are the notes Conrad made about leeches.

Used in medicine
Leeches have three 'jaws' to bite with
They inject an anaesthetic so they don't hurt you when they bite you
600 different species

Conrad used his notes to make the overall structure for the presentation. Look back to page 53 to remind yourself about how a presentation is put together from a list of points.

Look back to page 53

Copy pictures

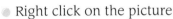

You can copy a picture from the Internet onto the clipboard of your computer, and then paste it into your own work. The pupils decided to copy this picture into their *mini-beasts* project file.

If you want to copy a picture from the Internet into a file of your own (for example a presentation):

- Right click on the picture
- Pick **Copy**
- Open your file using the right software package
- Find the place where you want the picture to go
- **Paste** the picture into the presentation or document

Remember to consider copyright issues.

Download multimedia

Presentations can include sound and moving images as well as text and pictures. The Internet is a good source of sounds and moving images.

Click for a sound bite

Click here to listen to the WAV sound file

On the site about leeches the pupils found this sound clip. The clip is available in two sound file formats. WAV is the file format you looked at on page 61.

the file format you looked at on page 61

The *Windows* media player starts up, and the sound file is downloaded onto your computer.

- Right-click on the sound to save it as a file onto your computer. Then you can use it in your presentation

On the next page you will also see some moving images available on the Internet.

Navigation

Remember that you can use these buttons on the web browser to move about between the sites you have seen.

WHAT YOU HAVE TO DO

As you look through the site for information, make notes and copy at least one picture into a document.

Type up the notes and put them together with the picture to make a short report on a topic of interest. Keep your work in your IT folder.

4. What ho, Jeeves?

There are millions of sites on the Internet. How can you find the Internet sites you need? The remainder of this unit is about finding useful web sites.

Searching for sites

Search engines are web sites where you type in key words or questions. They then display a list of links to sites relating to those keywords.

You should already know how to use a search engine. On this page you will look at two different search engines and compare them. You will see how different search engines produce different results.

Try out the search engines shown on this page, investigating the topic of your choice.

Search topic

All the pupils in a class were studying insects. Peter Parker used a camera to take photos of spiders and spider webs in the school grounds. He put these together to make a display in the Science room.

The next week he spent the lesson searching the Internet for more information. The spiders he found in the school grounds had been small and harmless, but he knew that spiders in other countries could be deadly.

Peter picked *deadly tropical spiders* as the topic for this Internet search.

Ask Jeeves for Kids!

Ask Jeeves for Kids! is a specialist search engine designed for use by young people, for example to help with school work. The URL is

www.ajkids.com

Here is the question Peter typed

Click here to ask the question

When Peter clicked on the **Ask** button he saw the web site screen shown at the top of the next page.

Ask Jeeves can't answer the question exactly. But it suggests other questions that might be of interest.

The software on the web site has worked out that the two most important words in the original question were *spider* and *poison* and it offers some interesting links on both of these subjects.

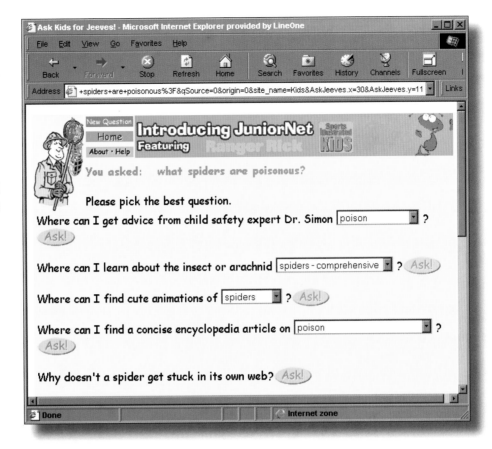

Follow a link

Peter clicked on the question *Where can I find cute animations of spiders?*. This was what he saw next.

You can't tell by looking in this book, but all these spider pictures are cartoons that move and scuttle about.

Peter bookmarked the site to think about later. A cartoon of a spider would be great to display on a computer screen. But, on the other hand, the files that store moving images are huge, and take a long time to download over the Internet.

Bookmarks

Remember that you can **bookmark** any site that you like, and then return to it later. Just click on this tool bar icon.

Find one site related to your chosen topic and bookmark it.

 103

5. Yahooligans

On the last page in this unit you will look at a new type of search engine. How does it contrast with others you have seen?

Yahooligans

After investigating *Ask Jeeves* the pupil decided to try another search engine. This was *Yahooligans* – the young people's version of a search engine called *Yahoo*.

Yahoo works in a quite different way to *Ask Jeeves*. Instead of presenting answers to questions it classifies web sites into categories. Here is the web site for *Yahooligans*. The URL for this site is

www.yahooligans.com

Printing

Don't forget you can print out an entire web site, both text and pictures, by clicking on this button. You probably don't want to do this too often – better to make notes and copy individual items such as pictures.

Always ask permission before printing.

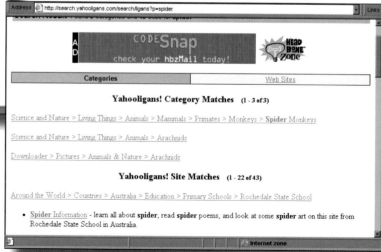

Search

Peter typed in *spider* as a keyword. When he clicked on **Search** he saw the screen shown on the right.

Yahooligans found three categories (spider monkeys, spiders, and pictures of spiders). You could click on one of these categories to find out more. It also found 43 individual web sites. On the next page is a list of some of them.

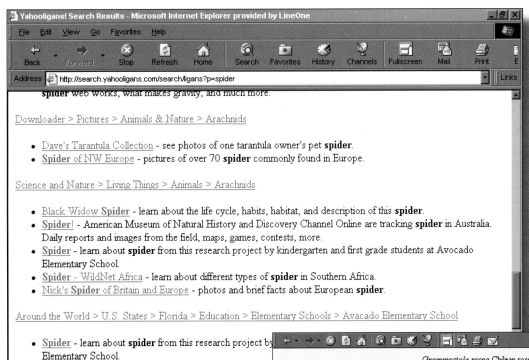

File Edit View Go Favorites Help

Back Forward Stop Refresh Home Search Favorites History Channels Fullscreen Mail Print E

Address http://search.yahooligans.com/search/ligans?p=spider Links

spider web works, what makes gravity, and much more.

Downloader > Pictures > Animals & Nature > Arachnids

- Dave's Tarantula Collection - see photos of one tarantula owner's pet **spider**.
- **Spider** of NW Europe - pictures of over 70 **spider** commonly found in Europe.

Science and Nature > Living Things > Animals > Arachnids

- Black Widow **Spider** - learn about the life cycle, habits, habitat, and description of this **spider**.
- **Spider**! - American Museum of Natural History and Discovery Channel Online are tracking **spider** in Australia. Daily reports and images from the field, maps, games, contests, more.
- **Spider** - learn about **spider** from this research project by kindergarten and first grade students at Avocado Elementary School.
- **Spider** - WildNet Africa - learn about different types of **spider** in Southern Africa.
- Nick's **Spider** of Britain and Europe - photos and brief facts about European **spider**.

Around the World > U.S. States > Florida > Education > Elementary Schools > Avacado Elementary School

- **Spider** - learn about **spider** from this research project by Elementary School.

Computers, Games, and Online > World Wide Web > Tutorial

Yahoo

Grammostola rosea Chilean rosehair

Chilean Rose tarantulas are for the most part slow and calm. They tolerate being handled and rarely flick hairs, this makes for a great choice as a first tarantula.

Look at the top link in this list – *Dave's Tarantula Collection*. Sounds interesting.

The pupil clicked on this link. He found a whole series of pictures, shown on the right.

If you want to look at this site, the URL is
http://www.geocities.com/Yosemite/2448/pictures.html

On Target

You should now know how to:

- use the Internet to enhance your work
- explore web sites with a critical eye
- obtain information in a variety of forms
- search effectively for the items you need.

WHAT YOU HAVE TO DO

Use the two search engines shown in this unit to search for web sites on your chosen topic.

Compare the results of the two search engines. Which was most useful to you?

8 Electronic Communication

In this unit you will learn how communication technologies are used to send and receive messages.

On Target

You should already know about:

- e-mail software packages
- how to send and receive e-mail
- sending computer files using e-mail.

In this unit you will learn about **communicating electronically** using:

- faxes
- video conferencing
- e-mail.

You will look in more detail at the software that is available to help you to send and receive e-mail. You will need to know how to:

- pick the most effective means of communication
- design communications to get your message across.

Sending messages

There are many ways of communicating messages. Some have been around for a long time. The three main ways that you may use are:

- speaking face-to-face
- writing letters
- talking on the telephone.

Now there is a greater range of methods you can use:

- send a fax
- page someone electronically
- video-conferencing
- e-mail.

Each of these methods has its advantages. There are times when you would use each method. There are times when a particular method is not appropriate.

IT at work

Nowadays police in the different regions of the country co-operate with each other, and with police forces all over the world, to share information. Sometimes it is essential to send and receive messages instantly. Sometimes the messages must include pictorial information – photos of suspects, identikit pictures, and fingerprints for example. Sometimes other computerised information must be sent, such as the results of forensic analysis.

The new forms of electronic communication that are available nowadays help police to share evidence, and to track criminal organisations across international borders.

Face-to-face

Speaking face-to-face is the most natural method of communication, but obviously it is only suitable for people who are near to you.

If you rely on this type of communication you might have to travel around a lot. An example is a salesman who has to drive to meet clients.

● Why do you think a salesman might prefer to communicate face-to-face?

Letter-by-letter

Lots of communication is done by letter. The main disadvantage of using letters is that it takes a long time for the letter to arrive. You can't send a message and get an answer the same day.

● What was the last letter (or card) you sent by post? Could you have used any other type of communication instead?

Post early for Christmas?

On the phone

People communicate by talking on the telephone. This is quick and easy. Of course, when you are using the phone, you can only communicate in speech. You can't show somebody a picture or a plan.

● What was the last phone call you made or received? Were you able to get the message across?

● What are the advantages of having a mobile phone?

Faxes

By using a fax you can send a picture or a document over the telephone line. The fax machine scans the document, just like a photocopier. Then it sends the signals that make the picture down the telephone to another fax machine. The second fax machine prints out a copy of the document.

● Have you ever sent or received a fax? Why was a fax the best way of sending the message?

Using a pager

A pager is a device that will send a very simple message to someone. If you want to contact someone with a pager you use a telephone to ring them up. You won't be able to speak to them however.

Instead the pager will make a sound and display a simple message using numbers. The person you've paged then needs to find a telephone to call you back.

Of course it's possible to send messages using a number code instead. So, for example 180 might mean *come back home*. Some pagers can show a short dictated text message.

● In what situations do you think it might be particularly useful to have a pager? Think about when someone might not want to have a mobile phone switched on.

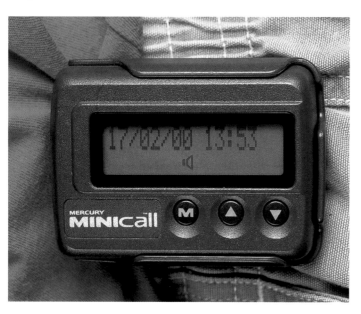

E-mail

E-mail is short for electronic mail. E-mail is sent down the same links that join computers to the Internet. When you use e-mail you write a message on your computer. You send the message to somebody else's computer. When they have time they can look at your message.

E-mail is a flexible method of communication with many advantages. It has lots of extra features. You will learn more about e-mail on page 114.

Video-conferencing

One disadvantage of using the phone is that you can't see the other person's face. Seeing the other person's expression can help communication.

A videophone has a little screen and a camera. By looking at the little screen you can see the face of the person you are talking to, and they can see you.

● Can you think of any disadvantages of being able to see as well as talk on the phone?

Video-conferencing is an extension of this idea. Instead of just two people talking on the phone a whole group of people can be connected. Everyone can see everyone else's face. Companies use this system to hold a meeting without everybody having to travel. It is much cheaper than paying for everyone to drive or take the train to the meeting place.

Good communication

You've learned about how to make good documents. You have to take into account:

- the audience for the document
- the information you want to communicate
- the impression you want to give.

It is the same when you send a communication.

Try to put yourself in the place of the person who will read your communication.

- Have you told them everything they need to know?
- Have you expressed it in a way they will understand?

Think about the impression you will make.

- Is your communication polite?
- Are you communicating to a friend, or a stranger?
- Should your communication be formal or informal?

The sign of a good communication is that you get the results you want. If you want the answer to a question, a good communication is one that gets you the answer. A polite and friendly request is much better than a rude and abrupt demand. Learn more about effective communication on page 112.

In this introduction you have seen the wide range of communication methods that are available. One of the skills of effective communication is to pick the right method (for example, should you phone? Should you send a fax?)

Learn more about picking the right method of communication on the next page.

What other unusual ways of sending messages can you think of?

Getting IT Right in...

Modern Languages

In any subject where you have to ask outside the school for information, you should consider each of the available means of communication.
Face-to-face requests and letters should not be forgotten, but sometimes electronic methods of communication are the most useful.

Pupils in a class learning French communicated with French pupils using e-mail. This is an alternative to having *pen friends* who write letters. The main advantage was that it is much quicker to send an e-mail than to send a letter.

WHAT YOU HAVE TO DO

1. Think of a question that you would like to ask a famous person.

2. Write down the question. Try to express it in a way that is polite. Remember that the sign of good communication is that you get the response you want.

3. How would you ask this question to the famous person? What method would work best? Would you ask it over the phone or perhaps send an e-mail?

Put the text of the question, and your notes on the method you would use, in your IT folder.

I. Am I making myself clear?

On this page you will see how to pick the right type of communication.

Picking the right method

In the introduction to this unit you saw that there are several different ways of communicating a message. Here you will look at the advantages and disadvantages of the different methods. You will think about the circumstances when it is right to use each method.

You will look at examples of communication by young people. Try to relate what you learn to your own experiences. Try to think about what you would do.

Get the picture?

Sometimes you need to send a picture or a diagram to someone.

What methods can you use?

● You can send a picture in a letter.

● You can send a copy of a picture by fax.

● You can send a picture as a computer file with an e-mail.

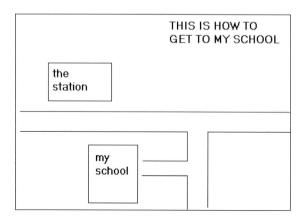

THIS IS HOW TO GET TO MY SCHOOL

the station

my school

Sending a picture by letter is easy. Put it in an envelope, and pop it in the post. The main disadvantage is that the picture probably won't get there until the next day.

A fax will get there straightaway. But you can only send a fax if both of you have a fax machine. Most people don't have a fax machine at home.

An e-mail is quick too. Anyone who is attached to the Internet can receive an e-mail. But you can only send a picture by e-mail if it is in the form of a computer file.

So how do you decide which method to use? Think about these questions.

● How urgent is it?

● What equipment does the other person have?

● What form is the picture in?

Talk or text?

Do you want to say your message? Or do you want to write it down? This makes a big difference to the kind of communication that you can use.

● If you want to talk to the other person then you will have to meet them, or phone them.

● If written text will do, then think about fax or e-mail.

Talking is more friendly and personal. But when you write a message you have time to think about it.

i Attaching a file *p117* Video conferencing *p108*

Some types of communication can be a bit annoying. When the phone rings it interrupts what you are doing. Other types of communication are less of a problem. For example, you can wait until you are ready to read an e-mail.

When it is important not to interrupt and when you don't want to be annoying, consider a form of communication other than the telephone.

Example 1

Michelle and Tina were both fans of the same pop group. The two girls lived in different towns and only saw each other once a month. They went together to a concert. One girl bought a programme. She wanted to give a copy of this programme to her friend.

- What methods could she use?
- What are the advantages and disadvantages of each method?

Example 2

Owen had gone on holiday, when he remembered some homework that was very late. He knew he would get into trouble if he didn't send it straightaway to his teacher. The homework was finished. All he had to do was send it.

- When you are away from home, it can be difficult to send messages. What would you do in this situation?

Example 3

Daljit was watching a programme on the TV. There was a quiz, with the chance to win a computer games console that he really wanted. He knew the answer to the question. But how should he send the message?

Phoning would be quick. But would the line be engaged? Have you ever tried phoning with the answer to a TV quiz?

He could send a letter. But how long would that take? Would it get there in time?

The TV programme gave an e-mail address. Perhaps he could send an e-mail with the answer?

- Have you ever entered a quiz of this kind? What method did you use? Which do you think is the best method?

Example 4

Mr Meredith was working on an oil rig. Often he didn't see his family for months. He wanted to keep in touch with his children. He sent letters and phoned whenever he could.

The oil company gave the man the opportunity to use video-conferencing. This meant he could see his children and his wife while he spoke to them.

- If you were living far away from somebody you cared about, how would you like to communicate?
- What are the advantages of seeing the person you are speaking to?
- Many people say they wouldn't like a videophone. Can you think of a good reason why not?

WHAT YOU HAVE TO DO

1. **Look at all the examples on this page. In each case think of the method of communication that you would recommend.**

2. **Write down the method you would choose in each case. Make sure you mention the advantages and disadvantages of the method.**

Put what you have written in your IT folder.

2. Being conventional

On this page you will look at the content of your communication. You need to design your communications to get the results you want?

Safe, polite, effective

It is easy to tell if your communication has been **effective**. If you get the result that you want, then it was a good communication. On this page you will look at ways to get the results you want.

How can you structure your communication to make sure that you:

- get the message across
- make a good impression
- keep yourself safe?

Look at some examples and think about what you would do in the same situation.

Conventions ■

There are conventions about how to use the different methods of communication. If you learn these conventions then it is easier to make your communication effective.

You have probably learned the formal conventions of letter writing at school. For example, putting the date in the top left corner of the letter, and starting with *Dear... .*

There are different conventions when you send e-mail, answer the phone, or send faxes.

Cover sheets ■

When you send a fax you normally send a cover sheet with it. This is a kind of front page that you send before the main fax.

The cover sheet should say:

- who you are
- the subject of the fax
- who the fax is for
- the number of pages in the fax.

By looking at the cover sheet the person who receives the fax can check that the entire fax is received and then pass it on to the right person.

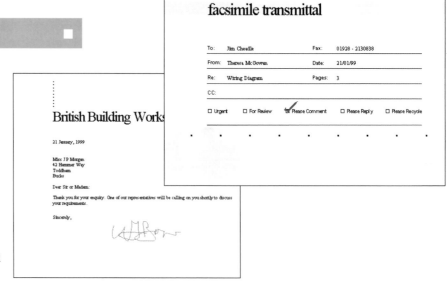

- If you were faxing your computer studies homework to your teacher, what would you put on the cover sheet?

E-mail conventions ■

E-mail is almost always written in an informal style. Instead of starting with *Dear Sam* you might start with *Hi Sam*. Instead of ending with *Yours sincerely* you might end with *Bye*.

When you reply to an e-mail you often quote it in your reply. This makes it easier to understand.

An e-mail between two school friends. Never ask someone you don't know to your house

People try to keep e-mails brief. They try to say what they mean as simply as possible. To make e-mail even simpler, people use abbreviations instead of writing words out in full. Here are some examples:

AFAIK – as far as I know

ROFL – rolling on the floor laughing

BTW – by the way

One problem with e-mail is that people cannot see your face. Because the e-mail is so short and informal there is a danger that people will misunderstand each other. For this reason people sometimes put little *faces* into their e-mails. These faces are supposed to show how you are feeling. They are sometimes called **smileys** or **emoticons**.

:-)	a happy face	:-(	a sad face
:-0	a surprise face	:-*	giving a kiss

Turn the page sideways if you want to see the *smileys*.

On the safe side ■

It is easy to send and receive e-mails. But unless you have met the other person you don't really know what they are like. Unfortunately people don't always tell the truth about who they are, and it is very difficult to check.

Below are some rules to help you to be safe.

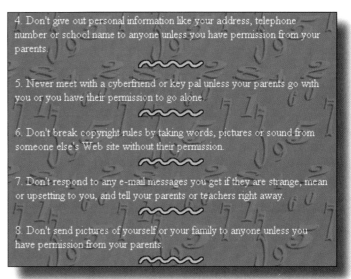

Some of the rules about e-mail safety from the **Kidscom** site (see page 99). Do you agree with them? Check out the full list on the Internet at **www.kidscom.com**

Politeness ■

Whatever method of communication you choose, it is important to be polite. You are more likely to get the response you want if you ask nicely.

Remember, the person you are writing to might have lots of other things to do. Make them want to help you.

WHAT YOU HAVE TO DO

Using a word processing program, create a blank fax cover sheet. There should be space for all the different items of information that need to be found on a fax cover sheet.

3. On the lookout

On this page you will learn how to use the software that lets you write and send e-mails.

Using e-mail software

If you have an Internet connection then you can use it to send e-mail messages. Next you will look at the software and learn how to write and send e-mails. You will look at e-mail addresses and how to use them.

You will also see how school pupils made use of e-mail. Try to follow the work using your own software.

E-mail addresses

Every e-mail account in the world has its own address. If you know the address you can send an e-mail. Most e-mail addresses take this form.

Bob@lakeside.ac.uk

Bob – this is the name of the person you are writing to

@ – this symbol is pronounced *at*

Lakeside.ac.uk – this is the name of the computer server which connects him to the Internet

Look out for e-mail addresses. You may find them in newspapers and magazines, on TV or on the radio. Your family and friends, or your teachers, may give you their e-mail addresses.

Outlook Express

The software package used as an example on this page is called **Microsoft Outlook Express**. You may find this icon on the tool bar at the bottom of your computer screen.

There are several other e-mail programs, which look slightly different. However, they all work in much the same way. Whichever e-mail program you are using you should be able to follow the work on this page.

The *Outlook Express* window looks like this.

Tool bar   E-mails stored in a folder

Folders   The contents of one e-mail

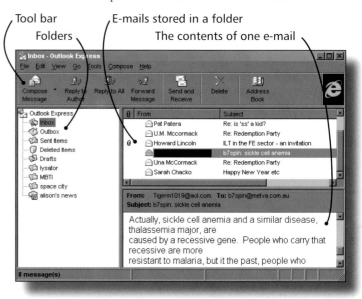

This e-mail program lets you store e-mails in folders. One folder is selected in this picture; you can see a list of the e-mails in that folder. The person who sent each e-mail is shown, and the subject of each e-mail. One of the e-mails is selected; you can see the full contents of that e-mail.

The tool bar contains icons that let you perform different actions.

You can move messages between folders by dragging them with the mouse.

E-mail conventions p113

Send an e-mail

If you want to send an e-mail:

● Click on this symbol on the tool bar

You will see a window like this one. It has its own tool bar. You will be using this later.

Enter the e-mail address here · · · · · · · · Type the e-mail here

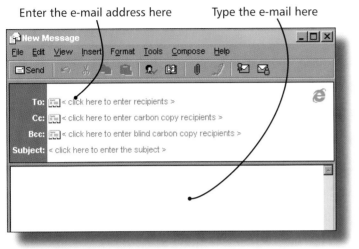

● Type the e-mail address at the top of the window

● Enter a subject in the space provided. Remember, when you see a list of e-mails you see the subject only, so make it a good explanation of the content

● Type the full e-mail in the main part of the window

● When you have finished the e-mail, click on this button

In most e-mail packages this will send the e-mail to a folder called the **Outbox**, where it is stored until you are ready to send it. But in some packages the e-mail might be sent immediately without going to an outbox first.

Connect and send

All e-mails you write will be stored in the **Outbox** folder. You have to connect to the Internet to send them to the right address.

● To send all the e-mails in the **Outbox**, click on this button

You might have to give a password to connect to the Internet. The computer will also check whether there are any e-mails waiting for you. If there are, it will download them so that you can read them.

Find out more about reading and replying to e-mails on the next page.

Sent Items

If you look back at the list of folders in the main window you will see one folder called **Sent Items**. Many e-mail packages have such a folder. All the e-mails you have sent are stored in this folder. You can look at the e-mails you have sent, and you can print them out.

Here is an example of a sent e-mail.

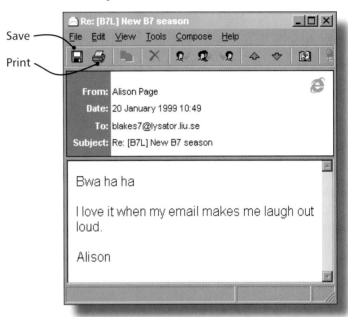

Look at the tool bar. When you look at an e-mail which has been sent you see this type of tool bar. There are icons which let you save and print the message. This is useful when you want to print out your work to hand it in.

Some e-mail packages do not allow you to look at copies of the e-mails you have sent. In this case you must save the e-mail to a file before you send it.

WHAT YOU HAVE TO DO

Your teacher will give you the e-mail address of another pupil in your class.

Compose an e-mail describing a software package that you have used, and send an e-mail to the address that you have been given.

Look in the Sent Items folder for the e-mail you have sent. Print a copy and put it in your IT folder.

4. The right to reply

On the last page in this unit you will see how to read the e-mails that you receive, and how to send replies to them.

Receiving and replying to e-mails

On the previous page you sent an e-mail to someone in your class. That means that someone should have sent an e-mail to you. On this page you will see what happens when you receive an e-mail and how you can read it and reply to it. Try to follow the work on this page using your own software package.

Send and receive

When you click on the **Send and Receive** icon you connect to the Internet. The e-mails in your outbox folder are sent on their way. When the computer has finished sending out the e-mails, any e-mails addressed to you are copied onto your computer.

The e-mails that have been sent to you are stored in the **Inbox** of your computer.

Read e-mails

All the e-mails that you have received will be listed in the **Inbox** folder.

● Double-click on an e-mail to read it in full. It will be displayed in a window like this one

Look at the tool bar. You have seen this tool bar before. It is the one that appears over any e-mail which has already been sent. You can use it to save or print the e-mail.

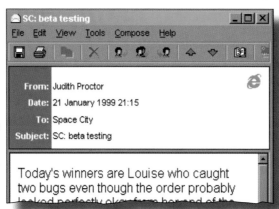

Reply

It is easy to **reply** to an e-mail.

● Click on this button on the tool bar

Your package may show this button without a picture. The computer automatically makes a **reply** e-mail, which might look something like this.

The reply has these features:

● it is automatically addressed to the person who wrote the e-mail

● it has the same subject line, with *Re:* in front of it

● it has all the text of the original e-mail, with this symbol > in front of each line.

Of course, you can make changes to any of these features. In particular, you should delete most of the quoted text, just leaving the essential lines. If you don't do this then your reply could get very long.

Forwarding

You can also **forward** an e-mail to another person. You shouldn't do this without permission, or if the e-mail is private or personal.

● To forward click on this button

The computer automatically makes a forwarded message that looks something like this.

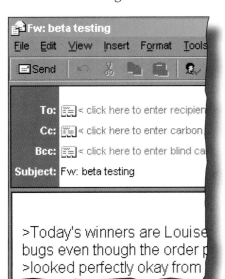

The forwarded message has these features:

● the text of the original is quoted
● the subject is the same, with *Fw* in front of it
● there is no e-mail address shown, you have to enter one.

Attachments

When you make a new e-mail, or reply to or forward one you can attach a computer file to it. The file is sent down the phone line together with the e-mail. The person who receives the e-mail receives a copy of the file. They can use it on their own computer.

To attach a file to an e-mail click on this button with a picture of a paper clip. You will see a window like this one.

It is just like an **open** or **save** window. Locate the file and click on the **Attach** button.

An e-mail with a file attached looks like this.

If you receive a file with an attachment, double-click on the attachment to open it up, or save it on your own computer system.

On Target

You have now completed the unit on electronic communication. You should know how to:

■ pick a suitable form of electronic communication
■ design a message using the correct conventions
■ send and receive e-mail messages.

WHAT YOU HAVE TO DO

You should have received at least one e-mail from another pupil in your class.

1. **Forward the e-mail you received to your teacher.**

2. **Reply to the e-mail.**

Print out the e-mail you received, and the reply you sent. Put the print-outs in your IT folder.

9 Spreadsheets

This unit is all about spreadsheet software. This software is used to help with all work involving numbers. A spreadsheet will store the numbers you enter, it will work out calculations for you, and it will create graphs to show your results.

On Target

You should already know how to:

- enter numbers and words into a spreadsheet
- use simple formulas to work out results
- make graphs from the numbers in a spreadsheet.

In this unit you will revise these skills and learn how to:

- use spreadsheets to solve problems
- find out facts and use them to build a spreadsheet
- save time by copying values and formulas
- vary values and explore change.

You will see how some pupils used spreadsheet software to help with their work. This will show you some new spreadsheet skills, and give you some ideas about how you can use spreadsheets to help with your own schoolwork.

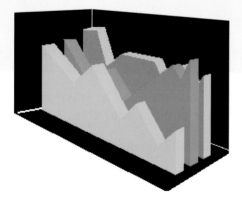

Values, labels and processes ■

When you perform a calculation you take **starting values**. You **process** these values through various operations (such as addition and multiplication) and you end up with results. When you set out the calculation you usually add **labels** to show what all the values mean.

Title

Starting values

Shopping List

Bread rolls   68p
Milk   48p
Jam   £1.89
Bacon   £2.10
Frozen chips   £1.29
Tea bags   £1.25
Chocolate   75p

Labels

TOTAL   £8.44

Process (addition)

Result

IT at work

Most small and medium sized businesses use spreadsheet packages to prepare business accounts. For example a business will use a spreadsheet when planning a new venture.

By using a spreadsheet, the person in charge can see how much the new plan will cost, and how much new revenue they can hope to raise.

Business Plan *for Microsoft Office*

- Present your thoughts in a professional, polished manner
- Communicate with colleagues and clients more effectively
- Save hours of time on formatting, inputting, and fussing
- Take maximum advantage of Windows 95 technology

This software company creates spreadsheets for businesses. The structure and layout of the spreadsheet has already been set up. All the person has to do is enter the facts and figures for their particular company

A spreadsheet is a piece of software that lets you enter starting values and the formulas to carry out operations. The software will perform the calculation for you and display the results. Better than working sums out on paper?

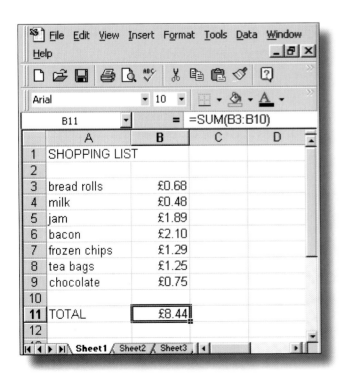

The same calculation set out using a spreadsheet

So why use a spreadsheet to help with your schoolwork? What advantages does it have, compared to doing the work by hand, with paper and pen?

Of course, the spreadsheet offers the same advantages as a word processor, such as neatness and the chance to make corrections without making a mess.

But a spreadsheet has other advantages too. The biggest advantage is a simple one – it will do your sums for you. You tell it what sum to do, and it will give you the answer immediately.

Better than a calculator?

But, you may say, why not use a calculator instead? That works out answers for you.

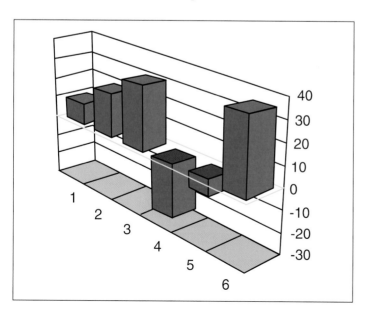

One advantage of a spreadsheet over a calculator is that it doesn't just give you the results of your sums.

- It sets them out in a neat way.
- It lets you generate graphs.

But an even bigger advantage of using a spreadsheet instead of a calculator is that it lets you **try things out**. It lets you answer the question **What if...?**

What if...?

Earlier you saw how a calculation has **starting values** and **processes**. In a shopping list the starting values were the cost of each item. The process was adding all the costs together.

Once you have set up a spreadsheet you can make changes to the starting values. The spreadsheet will work out the new results automatically.

The person using the shopping list tried out some new values. She only had £10.00. Could she afford to buy the expensive chocolate she wanted, costing £1.99, and twice as much milk, costing 96p?

As she discovered from the spreadsheet, the answer is no, not unless she economised in some other area.

You can sit down at a spreadsheet and try out lots of different values, and see what the results are. The spreadsheet will do the working out for you, giving you time to think about the content of your work.

Getting IT Right in...

Design & Technology

Pupils designed and made laminated plastic place mats from magazine pictures of film stars.

A suitable dinner companion?

They used a spreadsheet package to evaluate the production cost of the place mats, and to work out how much they would need to charge in order to make a profit.

	A	B
1	PRINTED PLACE MATS	
2		
3	Costs	
4		
5		per 100
6	Reinforced card	£ 60.00
7	Printing	£ 120.00
8	Lamination	£ 75.00
9	Total costs	£ 255.00
10		
11	Sales	
12		
13	Selling price	£ 3.00
14	Quantity	100
15	Total income	£ 300.00
16		
17	Profit/Loss	£ 45.00
18		

Trying things out

You have seen in earlier units how computers can help you to experiment and try things out. You have seen how you can try different styles and effects. You have seen how you can make 'drafts' of work (see page 9).

Spreadsheets should help you to take risks and be a bit more daring in the things you try to do:

- it is less risky, because you can correct mistakes without wasting time or making a mess
- it is easier, because the spreadsheet will let you try out lots of different versions, with hardly any extra work
- by taking some of the time and effort out of calculations the spreadsheet should give you time for exploring and learning new things.

Here are two examples:

- while his friends were slowly colouring in graphs with felt tip pens, Christopher created four different graphs using a spreadsheet package
- while her friends were still working out the cost of ingredients for a batch of biscuits, Jay had thought of a new recipe, and worked out that it would be even cheaper to make.

WHAT YOU HAVE TO DO

Four pupils have four different problems: how could a spreadsheet help each of these pupils? Write a short piece of advice for each one.

1. **Laura had to add up a long list of numbers, but each time she did it she got a different result.**

2. **Siobhan had to draw a graph for Geography, but it looked really scruffy.**

3. **Arpal had to work out the same results for ten different experiments in science, doing the same calculation over and over again. He was bored with it.**

4. **Tim was interested in making toys, but he hated working out the amount of materials he would need, so he kept putting it off.**

Keep your work in your IT folder.

I. Measuring up

On this page you will see how a spreadsheet was used to help with a school project.

Home insulation

Laura, Siobhan, Arpal and Tim worked with a spreadsheet package to help them with their work on a project.

You will see how they:

- entered values
- entered labels
- formatted a spreadsheet
- used formulas to work out results.

Try to do the same work that you see on this page, using your spreadsheet package.

Microsoft *Excel*

The package used as an example in this unit is **Microsoft *Excel***. There are several other well known spreadsheet packages. There are also several versions of *Excel*.

Microsoft
Excel

The spreadsheet you use at school may not be exactly the same as the one described here, but you will still be able to do the same work.

The project

The pupils were investigating energy saving and conservation. One thing they investigated was how insulating a house would save energy by reducing heat loss.

In this unit you will look at how they used spreadsheets to help them to investigate the topic.

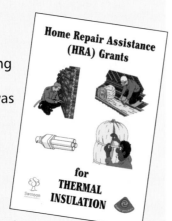

Home Repair Assistance
(HRA) Grants

for
THERMAL
INSULATION

Measuring area

The first thing the pupils did was to look at how a building loses heat. As you may know, it loses heat through the walls, floor and ceiling. But the worst heat loss is through the windows. The greater the surface area of the windows, the more heat is lost.

The pupils measured the height and width of all the windows in their classroom. They put these measurements into a spreadsheet package.

This is the spreadsheet that Siobhan made.

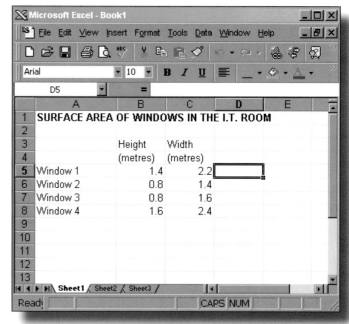

i A big investigation *p128*

Labels

The spreadsheet has plenty of **labels** so that you can understand it.

Answer these questions.

1. What is the subject of the spreadsheet?
2. What items are described in the spreadsheet?
3. What does the spreadsheet tell you about these items?
4. What measuring units were used?

Because the spreadsheet is well labelled you should be able to answer all these questions.

Formatting

To create the spreadsheet you just looked at, Siobhan entered labels and values. She also made some changes to the **format**.

- She increased the width of the first column.
- She formatted the title as bold text.

Values

There are two columns of **values**. The values are entered as numbers. It should be easy to tell what each value shows.

1. What number is shown in **cell C6**?
2. How do you think Siobhan found out this value?

Working out

Siobhan wanted to work out the surface area of each window. Area is calculated by:

*Height **times** Width.*

Here is the spreadsheet with the area of the first window calculated.

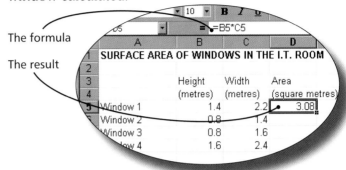

- To make the formula:
- Start with an *equals* sign
- Click on the *height* (in **cell B5**)
- Type the *multiply* sign (*)
- Click on the *width* (in **cell C5**)
- Click on the tick button to enter the formula and see the result

Completing the task

On the next page you will see how Tim extended the spreadsheet Siobhan had made. He put in a new formula to work out the total area of all the windows in the classroom.

Most heat loss in school is through the classroom window

WHAT YOU HAVE TO DO

1. **Create a spreadsheet that shows the height and width of all the windows in a room.**

2. **You can use the values shown on this page, or measure the windows in a real room (at school or at home). If you use a real room, pick one with several windows, not just one.**

3. **Format the spreadsheet by adjusting the column widths and making the main title bold.**

4. **Work out the surface area of the first window.**

2. Spreading the work

On this page you will see how the pupil extended the spreadsheet by using the copy feature and the sum function.

Extending the spreadsheet

On the previous page you saw how Siobhan created a spreadsheet to work out the surface area of windows in a classroom. This was part of a project about energy conservation.

Here you will see how Tim completed the spreadsheet, and found out the total size of the windows.

Try to do the same work that you see on this page. Load the spreadsheet file you created before, and work with it.

A trick to save time

The spreadsheet Siobhan made shows the area of one window. Tim wants to work out values for all the windows in the classroom. He has to do the same working out in each row. He wants to multiply width by height, each time.

Instead of typing four formulas, he can copy the first formula into all the other cells.

The cell with the formula is selected ready to copy it

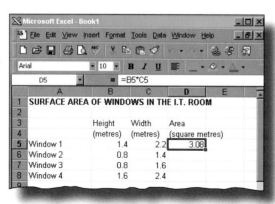

Next you will see how to do this.

Copy down

The cell with the formula is selected. Can you see the dot in the bottom right corner?

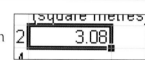

Find this dot

- Move the mouse pointer onto this dot and it should turn into a narrow black cross

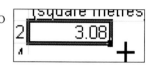

The mouse pointer turns into a black cross

- When you see the pointer change to a cross:
  - hold down the mouse button
  - drag the mouse over the next three cells
  - let go of the mouse button

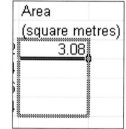

Drag the pointer over the empty cells

When you let go of the mouse button, the formula copies down into all the cells.

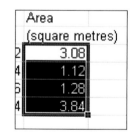

That's all you have to do to copy the formula.

Another method

If you find it difficult to make the previous method work, there is another method you can use. Use the ordinary mouse pointer for this.

- Drag the mouse pointer over the cell with the formula, and the cells below to select them
- Hold down the **Control** key
- Press the **D** key

This will copy the formula *down* to other cells.

Clever copying

The formula you copied looked like this. =B5*C5

But when it is copied into the cell below it changes to look like this. =B6*C6

In every row the formula changes, so that it works out the right answer.

- Look at the formulas in the different cells

Add up the total

Tim has worked out the area of each window. Now he wants to add up the total area of all the windows.

The first step is to add a label and select the cell where the answer is going to go.

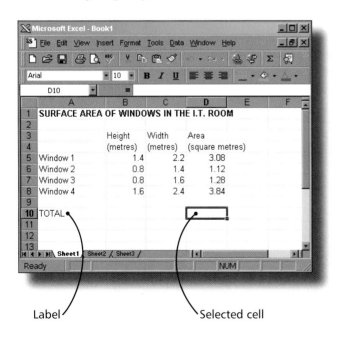

Label

Selected cell

We use the word *sum* to mean any working out. But in mathematical language, *SUM* means *add together a set of numbers*.

The mathematical symbol for *SUM* is Σ.

- Look carefully at the tool bar of the spreadsheet package and you should see this symbol
- Click on the *SUM* symbol

The computer works out what cells you want to add together, and marks them with a dotted line.

The *SUM* button

The computer will add up all these numbers

- Click on the tick button to accept the formula

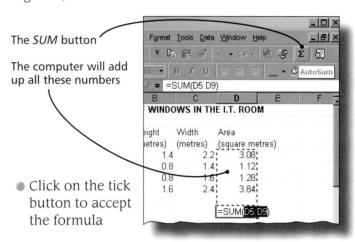

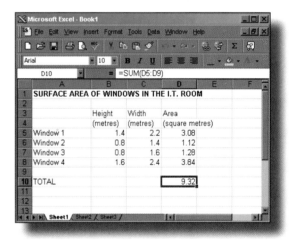

The spreadsheet is now completed.

3. Just suppose...

Here you will see how the pupils used the spreadsheet to test the effects of making changes.

What if...?

Next you will see how Laura extended the spreadsheet that Siobhan and Tim had made. She added a formula to work out the amount of heat that was lost through the classroom windows.

Arpal used the spreadsheet that Laura had made to work out how heat loss could be reduced by installing double-glazing. In other words he answered the question:

What if we double-glazed the classroom windows?

Try to do this work for yourself, using your own spreadsheet.

Heat loss

Heat loss is measured using units called **Watts**. You don't have to know what they are. Just understand that the bigger the number, the more heat is lost.

Heat loss is calculated by multiplying three values:

● the **surface area**
● the **temperature difference** between indoors and outdoors
● the **heat loss value** of the material used.

So to work out heat loss use this formula:

surface area × temperature difference × heat loss value.

Ordinary glass has a heat loss value of 6, which isn't very good. Double-glazing has a heat loss value of 2, so it is much better.

Set up the spreadsheet

The spreadsheet already shows the surface area of the windows. To work out heat loss you have to enter two new values:

● the temperature difference between indoors and outdoors
● the heat loss value of the windows.

Laura measured the temperature inside the classroom, and outdoors. The difference was 10°C.

Laura entered the heat loss value of 6, and the temperature difference of 10, into the spreadsheet. After she had typed in this information the spreadsheet looked like this.

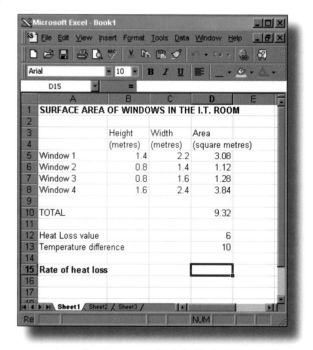

	A	B	C	D	E
1	SURFACE AREA OF WINDOWS IN THE I.T. ROOM				
2					
3		Height	Width	Area	
4		(metres)	(metres)	(square metres)	
5	Window 1	1.4	2.2	3.08	
6	Window 2	0.8	1.4	1.12	
7	Window 3	0.8	1.6	1.28	
8	Window 4	1.6	2.4	3.84	
9					
10	TOTAL			9.32	
11					
12	Heat Loss value			6	
13	Temperature difference			10	
14					
15	Rate of heat loss				
16					
17					

Remember all values must be labelled, as shown here

Work out the answer

After Laura had entered the three values she added a formula to work out the total heat loss. Remember the formula for heat loss is:

surface area × temperature difference × heat loss value.

Can you find these values in the spreadsheet?

- The surface area is shown in **cell D10**.
- The temperature difference is shown in **cell D12**.
- The heat loss value is shown in **cell D13**.

So the formula to work out heat loss value is:

= D10 * D12 * D13

Here is what the spreadsheet looked like after Laura entered the formula.

The formula

	D15		=	=D10*D12*D13
	A	B	C	D

	A	B	C	D
1	SURFACE AREA OF WINDOWS IN THE I.T. ROOM			
2				
3		Height	Width	Area
4		(metres)	(metres)	(metres)
5	Window 1	1.4	2.2	3.08
6	Window 2	0.8	1.4	1.12
7	Window 3	0.8	1.6	1.28
8	Window 4	1.6	2.4	3.84
9				
10	TOTAL			9.32
11				
12	Heat Loss value			6
13	Temperature difference			10
14				
15	**Rate of heat loss**			559.2
16				

The result

Remember that when you are entering a formula:

- start by typing an *equals* sign =
- select each value by clicking on it
- use an asterisk to multiply.

Print and save

Every time you enter a new value you create a new version of the spreadsheet.

- You might like to print each version of the spreadsheet.
- You might like to save each version using a different file name.

Look back to page 15 to remind yourself how to save with a new file name.

What if the room was double-glazed?

It seems that double-glazing a room would reduce heat loss. Arpal used the spreadsheet to check.

- Go to the spreadsheet and change the heat loss value to 2

This is what the spreadsheet looks like now.

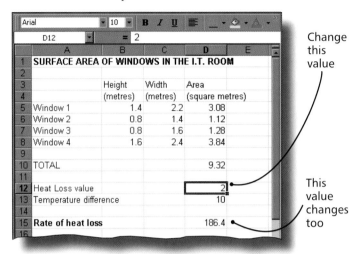

Change this value

This value changes too

When the new value was entered the computer recalculated the results.

This is one of the most useful features of spreadsheet packages. As soon as you change one of the values, the software works out a new answer.

WHAT YOU HAVE TO DO

1. **Add the heat loss and temperature values shown on this page to your spreadsheet.**

2. **Add a formula to work out heat loss.**

3. **Print and save the spreadsheet.**

4. **Change the values to show *what if* the windows had double-glazing.**

5. **Print the spreadsheet and save it using a new file name.**

6. **Look at the spreadsheets on this page and answer these questions.**

   - **What is the rate of heat loss without double-glazing?**

   - **What is the rate of heat loss with double-glazing?**

   - **How much difference does double-glazing make to heat loss?**

4. Out of the cold

On this page you will put together the skills you have learned to create a useful spreadsheet.

A big investigation

For the next stage of their project about heat loss and conservation the class looked at heat loss from a typical house.

Here you will see how Susannah used a spreadsheet to work out how heat was lost through different parts of a house, and how improved insulation could save energy.

Try to follow this work using your own spreadsheet package.

The bare facts

The teacher gave the class a set of facts about a typical house.

First she told them the surface area of a typical house:

Windows	**50 square metres**
Walls	**140 square metres**
Roof	**60 square metres**
Floor	**60 square metres**

Then she told them the heat loss values for the parts of the house:

Glass windows	**6**
Brick walls	**2**
Tile roof	**2**
Concrete foundations	**2**

Setting up the spreadsheet

Susannah used the facts to make this spreadsheet.

The spreadsheet shows all the facts. She left a space to put in the temperature difference and a formula to work out heat loss.

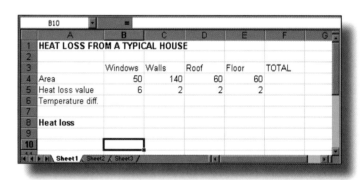

B10 =

	A	B	C	D	E	F	G
1	HEAT LOSS FROM A TYPICAL HOUSE						
2							
3		Windows	Walls	Roof	Floor	TOTAL	
4	Area	50	140	60	60		
5	Heat loss value	6	2	2	2		
6	Temperature diff.						
7							
8	Heat loss						
9							
10							

Sheet1 / Sheet2 / Sheet3

Completing the spreadsheet

Entering a formula

Susannah wanted to work out the heat loss through the windows. Remember that she had to multiply surface area, temperature difference and the heat loss value. If you need a reminder about this calculation, look back to the last page.

● The temperature difference between indoors and outdoors was 12°C. She entered it into the spreadsheet.

● She entered a formula to multiply the three values.

Here is the spreadsheet after Susannah had entered the formula.

B8 = =B4*B5*B6

	A	B	C
1	HEAT LOSS FROM A TYPICAL HOUS		
2			
3		Windows	Walls
4	Area	50	140
5	Heat loss value	6	2
6	Temperature diff.	12	
7			
8	Heat loss	3600	

Copying the formula

Remember that you can copy a formula to new cells. This is quicker than entering the formula lots of times. If you want to remember how to copy a formula, look at the *Copy Down* section on page 124.

Susannah has entered a formula to work out heat loss from the windows. She needs to copy this formula to work out heat loss from the walls, roof and floor.

Look at the spreadsheet you have made. Can you see where to copy the formula?

The formula is in **cell B8**. It needs to go into **cells C8**, **D8** and **E8**. That means Susannah must copy the formula to the **right**.

Use one of these methods.

Either

- Move the pointer to the corner of **cell B8**, until it turns into a black cross, and drag it to the right over the other cells

Or

- Select all the cells from **B8** to **D8** and press **Control** and **R** (to copy **Right**)

Calculating the total

Finally Susannah could add up all these values to work out total heat loss for the whole house.

- Select the cell where the **Total** belongs (**cell F8**)
- Click on the **SUM** button

The completed spreadsheet looked like this.

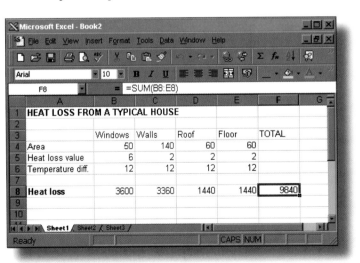

Investigating

If you insulate a house you can change the heat loss values:

Double glazing	**2**
Foam cavity walls	**0.5**
Felted roof	**0.5**

Susannah put these new values into the spreadsheet. She changed the title too.

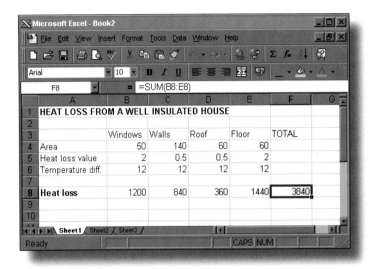

By swapping between the values she could investigate questions like these.

1. How much energy can you save by insulating a house properly?
2. If you could only make one change, which should you insulate – windows, floor or roof?

WHAT YOU HAVE TO DO

Produce a spreadsheet like the one shown on this page.

Use it to investigate the effect of insulation on heat loss.

Which type of insulation would you try first?

5. In the charts

On the last page of this unit you will learn how to make graphs from the values in a spreadsheet.

Graphs

In this unit you have seen how spreadsheets can be used to work out answers to questions. Here you will see how you can present spreadsheet answers in the form of **graphs**.

A graph is a good way of showing people the results of your spreadsheet. It looks interesting and colourful. Graphs are often easier to understand than lists of numbers.

The spreadsheet

All the graphs on this page are made from the spreadsheet you saw on the last page. It shows the heat loss from a house. The values can be changed to show the effect of insulating the house.

To make a graph:

● Select the cells with the labels and values you need

Sometimes this means you need to select two groups of cells.

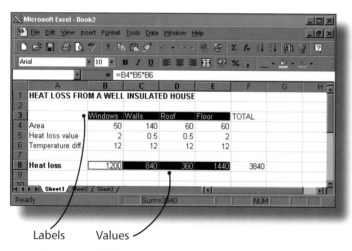

Labels   Values

To select two different groups of cells hold down the **Control** key while you drag the pointer over the cells.

Chart Wizard

Chart wizard is a function that lets you make graphs. You can find it on the tool bar.

● Start up chart wizard

You will see a window like this.

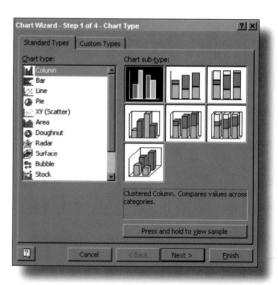

You can pick the type of graph you want from this window

By pressing the next and back buttons you can look through a whole series of chart wizard screens. Here is another example.

This screen lets you add a title to the graph. Each screen of the graph wizard lets you improve the graph

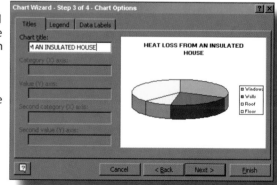

● When you have finished, click on **Finish**.

The graph is added to your spreadsheet.

You can resize and move it like any other graphic.

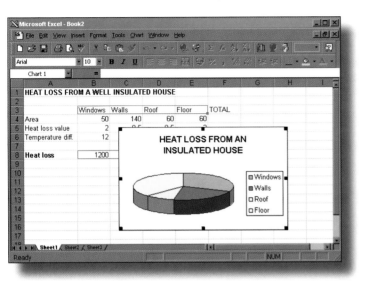

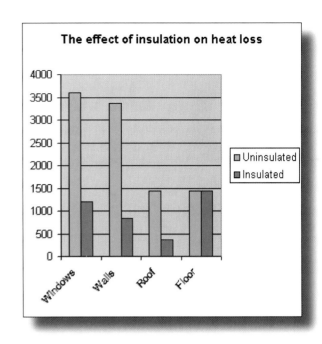

More graphs

On the right are some more graphs made by pupils in the class. Which do you like best? Which is worst?

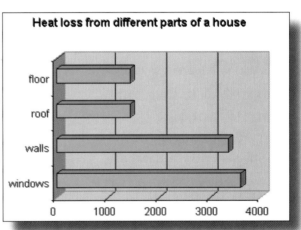

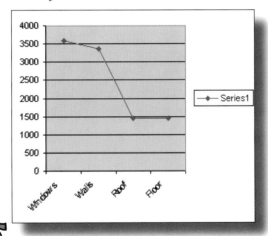

On Target

You have now completed the unit on the use of spreadsheets. You should know how to:

■ use spreadsheets to solve problems

■ find out facts and use them to build a spreadsheet

■ save time by copying values and formulas

■ vary values and explore change.

WHAT YOU HAVE TO DO

At the computer

1. Make two or more graphs from the values in your spreadsheet.

2. Print them out and put them in your IT folder.

Away from the computer

1. Look at your graphs with a critical eye. Which is best for showing the results?

2. Write a short evaluation of your graphs and put this in your IT folder.

10 Databases

A database is a structured collection of information stored on a computer system.

On Target

You should already know:

- how data is stored in a structured form
- how a data table is organised in columns and rows.

In this unit you will learn how to:

- set up a database to store data
- put data into a database
- make changes to a database
- extract answers from a database.

In these introductory pages you will look at how organising data makes it more useful.

Facts and figures

Sometimes next to a phone – in a house, or at work – there is a pad where people scribble down phone numbers and other important facts and figures.

These are raw facts and figures. They haven't been organised into any kind of structure.

Garbage In, Garbage Out

This is a well-known saying among computer users. It means that if the facts you put into the computer are wrong then the facts you get out of the computer will be wrong too.

People sometimes think that everything that comes out of a computer must be true. But everything in a computer was put there by people – and we all know that people can make mistakes, don't we?

You can say that again!

Organise facts and figures ■

When we store facts and figures we need to organise them. We place them in order, in a way that makes it easy to find the facts we need.

You can organise facts and figures on paper.

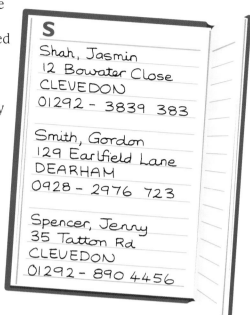

S

Shah, Jasmin
12 Bowater Close
CLEVEDON
01292 – 3839 383

Smith, Gordon
129 Earlfield Lane
DEARHAM
0928 – 2976 723

Spencer, Jenny
35 Tatton Rd
CLEVEDON
01292 – 890 4456

The facts from the phone pad shown on this page could be organised using an address book and an appointment diary.

- An address book – sorts facts in name order.
- An appointment diary – sorts facts in date order.

Data processing ■

Raw facts and figures in a disorganised state are called **data**. When data is organised to make it more useful it is called **information**. The action of turning data into information is called **Data Processing**.

How can you make information more useful? There are three main ways:

- organise the facts into a sensible order, like the words in a dictionary or the names in a phone book
- work out new facts from the ones you have. For example work out an average from a long list of numbers
- present the facts in an interesting way. For example print a report or a graph.

By now you have nearly finished working through this book, and you should have some ideas about how the computer can help you with all these **data processing** actions.

Processing numerical data is sometimes called *number crunching*

IT at work

If you don't know a phone number you can phone Directory Enquiries. The operator on the other end of the line has a database with all the phone numbers in the UK stored on it.

Each record in this database stores the information about one phone number.

The database probably has these fields in it.

- Area code
- Phone number
- Initial
- Surname
- Address fields
- Town, city or area

The operator can search the database by typing in a name and a town. The computer tells her the phone number of every person who matches the details she has typed.

Card filing

When you have a lot of facts to organise you sometimes use a **card file**.

For example, a doctor's receptionist might use a card file to store patient's details. A librarian might use a card file to store details of all the books in the library.

Every card in a card file has the same overall structure. Then each empty card is filled in with a different set of facts. Finally the cards are organised into a suitable order (such as order of book title).

For example, a pupil worked as a DJ in her spare time. She used a card file to record details of all her CDs.

Below is what an empty card looked like.

```
BEANY DISCO 2000
Long Play : Y/N
Title :
Artist :
Tracks :




Date acquired :
Cost :
```

On the right is what the cards looked like when they were filled in.

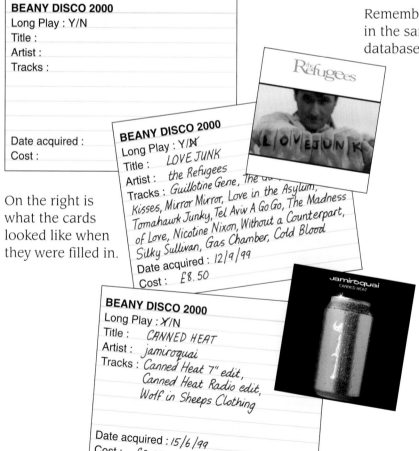

```
BEANY DISCO 2000
Long Play : Y/N
Title :    LOVE JUNK
Artist :   the Refugees
Tracks : Guillotine Gene, The ...,
Kisses, Mirror Mirror, Love in the Asylum,
Tomahawk Junky, Tel Aviv A Go Go, The Madness
of Love, Nicotine Nixon, Without a Counterpart,
Silky Sullivan, Gas Chamber, Cold Blood
Date acquired : 12/9/99
Cost :    £8.50
```

```
BEANY DISCO 2000
Long Play : Y/N
Title :    CANNED HEAT
Artist :   jamiroquai
Tracks : Canned Heat 7" edit,
        Canned Heat Radio edit,
        Wolf in Sheeps Clothing


Date acquired : 15/6/99
Cost :    £3.99
```

Computerised database

Instead of using paper and card to organise facts you can store them on a computer.

A **database** is a collection of facts stored as a computer file.

The data is stored in a structured form, similar to a card file. Once the data is in the computer you can organise it and look at it in lots of different forms.

On the next page of this unit you will see how data can be stored on a computer file.

Key terms

A database consists of **records**. Each record stores all the information on a particular person or thing.

● In a DJ database each record stores information about one CD.

A record is made up of **fields**. Each field is one piece of information.

● In a DJ database the title or cost of the CD would be one field.

Remember, all the records in a database are organised in the same structure. That means every record in the database has the same fields in the same order.

i Design the table *p138*   Enter records *p141*

Getting IT Right in....

Science

In a Science class pupils collected flowers and used a guidebook to identify them. They recorded facts about the flowers in a database. They stored details like these:

- the colour
- the number of petals
- the height of the plant
- the habitat
- the name of the flower
- the month in which it flowers.

Creating the database helped the pupils in two ways.

- In order to enter the data they had to find out the name of every plant. They learned a lot about identifying plants, and using reference material.
- Once the information was in the database they could use the information in many different ways. For example, they could easily print out the name of every yellow plant, or every plant that flowers in March.

Record structure

When data is stored in a database you can look at it one record at a time. Here is one record from the DJ database.

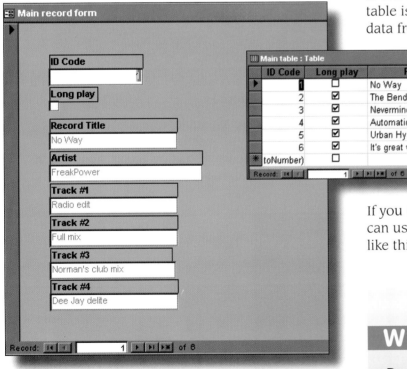

Table

Another way to show the information in a database is as a table.

A table looks like a spreadsheet. Each row of the table is one record in the database. Each column of the table is one field of the database. Here is a table of data from the same DJ database.

ID Code	Long play	Record Title	Artist	Track #1	
1	☐	No Way	FreakPower	Radio edit	Full mix
2	☑	The Bends	Radiohead	planet telex	the bend
3	☑	Nevermind	Nirvana	Smells like teen spirit	In bloom
4	☑	Automatic for the people	REM	Drive	Try not t
5	☑	Urban Hymns	The Verve	Bitter sweet symphony	Sonnet
6	☑	It's great when you're straight	Black grape	Reverend black grape	In the n.
toNumber)	☐				

If you don't have special database software, you can use a spreadsheet package to set up a data table like this.

WHAT YOU HAVE TO DO

Design an empty card that you could use to store the name, address and phone number of your family and friends.

Print out a couple of copies of the empty card and fill it in with details of two people that you know.

Put all of this information in your IT folder.

I. On the record

On this page you will look at an example of a database set up to help the DJ of a local disco.

A computerised database

Here you will look at a simple example of a computerised database.

The database file is called **Beany Disco 2000**. It is set up to store information about all the music CDs owned by a disco DJ.

Follow the instructions given here to start up the **Microsoft** *Access* software package, or whichever your school uses. There are many different software packages that let you create a computerised database.

Microsoft Access

Ask your teacher to prepare a database file you can load, and look at its main features.

Open the file ■

When you start up *Access* you are immediately asked whether you want to start a new database, or open an existing database.

Your teacher may have loaded the *Beany Disco 2000* database onto the school network, or some other storage area. You may see it in the list of available databases.

Click here to open *Beany Disco 2000*

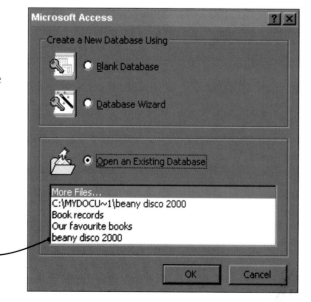

If you can't see *Beany Disco 2000* on the list then click on **More Files...**. You will see a familiar window like this.

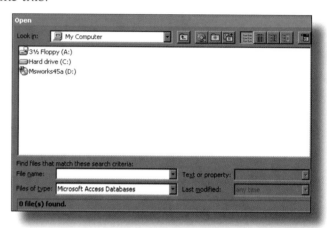

Use this window to open the file. Your teacher will tell you where it is stored.

Just two views are available, one **table** and one **record** form. Look back to page 135 to see the difference between a record-by-record view and a table view of a database.

Now you can look at the file you have opened.

i Table *p135* Records structure *p135*

Table view ■

When you open the database you will see a screen like this.

Click here to open the table

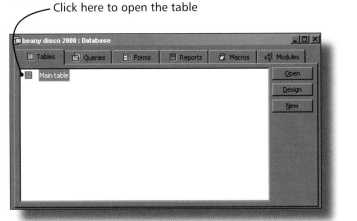

● Open the main table by clicking on the icon

Look on page 135 to see what the table looks like.

When you have finished looking at the table, click on the X in the top left corner to close down this view.

Artist	
FreakPower	Radio
Radiohead	planet

Record form view ■

Now you can look at the database using the **record form** view.

The **Forms** tab

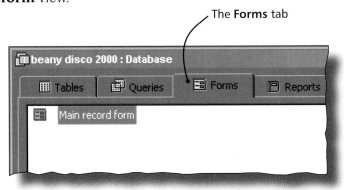

● Click on the **Forms** tab
● Open the *Main record form*

Look on page 135 to see what the record form looks like.

Close the record form when you have finished looking at it, by clicking on the X in the top right corner.

Fields

You have looked at the database in two ways – as a table and as a collection of separate records. Whichever view you choose you will have noticed the fields. Each field stores one piece of information (such as 'Artist' or 'Track #1').

Each field has its own field size and field type. When you make a new database on the next spread you will choose the size and type of each field in the database.

Field size

Each field has a certain amount of space in which you can enter information. 'Field size' is a number that tells you the amount of space available. 5 = space for five characters, 50 = space for fifty characters.

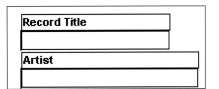

In this example the 'artist' field is a bigger size than the 'title' field

● What field sizes would you choose for 'artist' and 'title'?

Data type

In most fields you can type in any information. Such a field is called a 'text' field. But in other cases you can only enter particular kinds of information – a date for example, or a numerical value. Another field type is 'Yes/No' – a yes/no field can only store those two options.

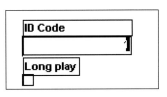

● What field types would you choose for 'ID code' and 'Long play'?

WHAT YOU HAVE TO DO

Open the *Beany Disco 2000* database and look at it in both record and table form.

2. A good read

On this page you will learn how to create a new database to store information on the computer.

Create a new database

A group of pupils created a database to store reports of the books they had read.

- They decided what facts they wanted to store.
- They started a new database file.
- They created an empty table with fields for each fact they wanted to store.

Here you can see what they did. Try to follow the work yourself using a database package.

The example

As part of their work for English, pupils were asked to write short reports on the books they read. They decided to create a database to summarise this information.

What information?

The pupils talked together about what information they needed to store. Here is what they decided on:

- book title
- author first name
- author surname
- type of book
- comments
- reviewed by
- review date
- star rating.

Their teacher suggested they also ought to have a *code* for each book report in the database.

Start a blank database

When you start up *Access* you are given the opportunity to start a new database, or load an existing database. If you are already working in *Access* then you will see these familiar icons on the tool bar.

- Start a blank database and give it a suitable file name and storage location

Start a table

The new blank database has no tables, no records, no information. A good place to start is to make a table ready to enter data. You will see this window.

Make sure the **Tables** tab is selected   Click on **New**

There are a number of different ways to create a new table.

- Choose **Design View** and click **OK**

i   Data type *p137*   Field size *p137*

Design the table

When you pick **Design View** you see a blank design screen. This is where you will enter the names of all the fields you want in the database.

The first field is 'Book Report Code'.

● Type this in the first cell of the database

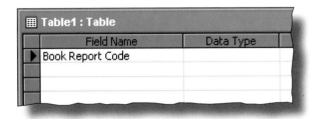

When you press the **Enter** key you will see the data type and field size. These are set automatically by the computer.

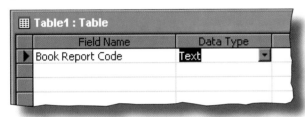

Adjust the database

You can make various changes to the database fields. For example you can:

● change the **data type**, so that the fields don't all store text data
● change the **field size**, so that some fields have more space than others.

You can explore these changes for yourself if you have time.

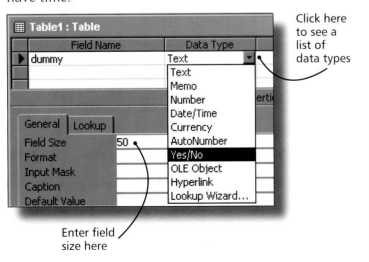

Click here to see a list of data types

Enter field size here

Save and exit

● Click on the **Save** icon and enter a name for the table you have created

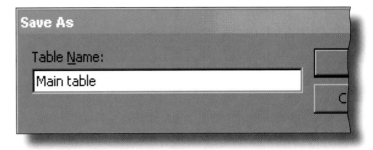

● Exit from the table design window in the usual way

The table you have just designed is now shown in the main database screen.

If you want you can open the blank table and start typing in records right away.

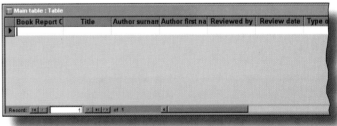

WHAT YOU HAVE TO DO

Create a book database like the one described on this page. Work in a group, and make decisions together about the fields to use.

3. A wonderful wizard

On this page you will see how to add records to a database.

Add data to the database

To put information into the database the pupils:

- created an input form
- used the form to enter data.

Here you can see what they did. Try to follow the work yourself using a database package.

Create a new form

On the last page you created a database with a single table. A table displays a whole set of records, set out like a spreadsheet.

Here you will create a record form. A record form displays one record at a time. You can also use it when you want to enter records.

- Make sure the database is open
- From the main view select the **Forms** tab
- Click on **New**

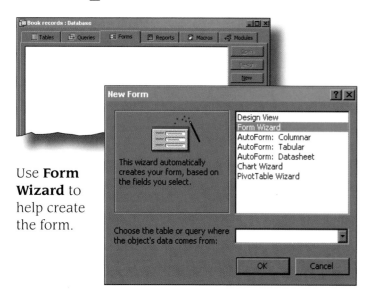

Use **Form Wizard** to help create the form.

Which fields?

You want the form to show all the fields you put in the table.

- Pick all the fields and click on the **Next >** button

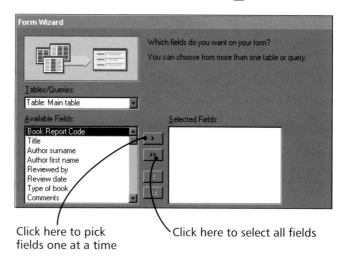

Click here to pick fields one at a time

Click here to select all fields

Pick a layout

Use the next screen of the Wizard to choose the overall **layout** of the form. For example, the form could show the fields one above the other. This is called the **Columnar** style.

This example shows the columnar style. Try out some of the others if you have time.

Pick a design ◼

You can use the other screens of the Form Wizard to pick a **design** for the form. Experiment with these, and see what style you like best.

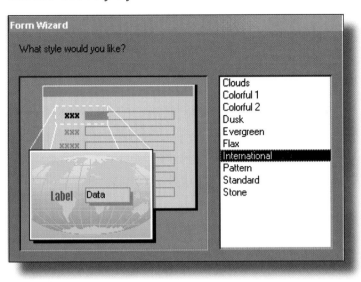

You will also have the opportunity to give the form a name. The pupils chose the name *Enter book reports*.

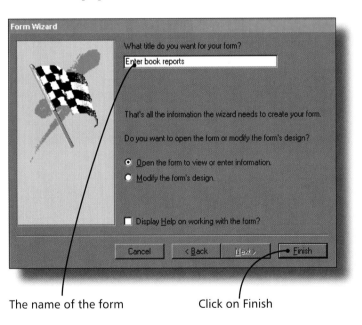

The name of the form   Click on Finish

Enter records ◼

Once they had made the record form the pupils could use it to enter book reports, one at a time.

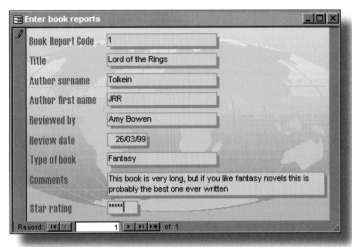

The final field in this form is 'Star Rating'. The pupils entered from 1 to 5 asterisks in this field to show how much they liked the book. When you have completed the last field on the form, press **Enter** and a new blank form comes up.

When you have entered all the records, close the form.

Printing ◼

You can print out the database at any time, using any form or table you have made.

● Load the **view** that you want to use
● Find the **print** icon on the menu bar

WHAT YOU HAVE TO DO

Create a record form to add records to the book database.

Everyone who is working together on this project should use the record form to add at least one record to the database. Pick a book you have read recently and create a record about that book.

4. Star quality

On the final page of this unit you will see how you can take information out of a database, for example to answer questions.

Report results

Here you will see how you can extract **answers** from a database by:

- looking at tables of data
- creating reports to display results.

Look at data in a table

The easiest way to look at the contents of a database is to open the Main Table. You will see all the data set out like a spreadsheet.

Create a report

You can create an attractive report to present selected data in a neat format.

- From the main database window, select the **Reports** tab and click on the **New** button.

The **Report Wizard** will make it easy for you to create a report.

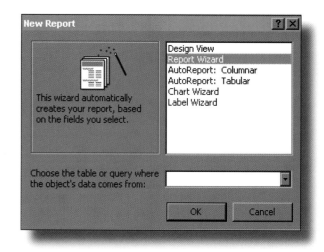

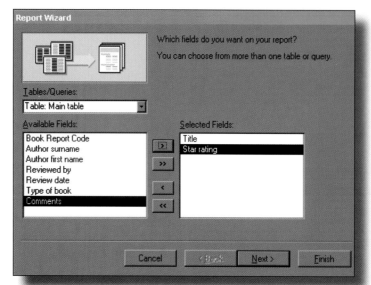

First select the fields that you want to show in the report. In this example the pupils have decided to show just the title of each novel, together with its star rating.

 i Table view *p137*

The Report Wizard lets you pick many different factors, including the style of the report.

As with all Wizards you can move backwards and forwards through the screens, making changes until you are satisfied.

When you click on **Finish** you will see the completed report.

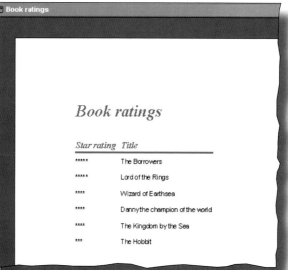

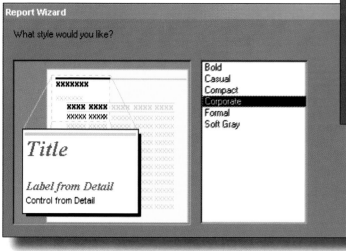

Remember, when you are looking at the report, you can print it out by clicking on the **print** icon.

More complex databases

The example databases you have looked at in this book were simple. There was one table, one record form, and one report.

Modern databases often have lots of different record forms and reports. By choosing a different form or report you can look at the data in a different way.

Modern databases often have lots of different tables. Each table stores different data. For example, a library database might store facts about borrowers in one table, and facts about books in another table. A third table would relate the two together, showing which people had borrowed which books.

A database like this, where there are many related tables, is called a **relational** database.

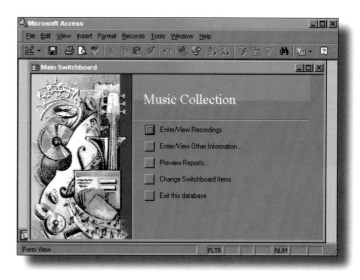

On Target

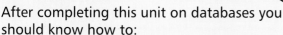

After completing this unit on databases you should know how to:

- set up a database structure
- store information in a database
- take useful information from a database.

WHAT YOU HAVE TO DO

Create two reports from your *book review* database.

- **One report should list the book titles and star ratings.**

- **The second report should list the book titles and authors.**

Index